MAN
AND THE ZODIAC

BY THE SAME AUTHOR

THROUGH THE EYES OF THE MASTERS
ADEPTS OF THE FIVE ELEMENTS

ARIES TAURUS GEMINI CANCER LEO VIRGO LIBRA
(Larger versions of these can be found on pgs. 212–215. — Publisher's note)

SCORPIO SAGITTARIUS CAPRICORN AQUARIUS PISCES

THE TWELVE SIGNS OF THE ZODIAC

[*Frontispiece*

MAN AND THE ZODIAC

By
DAVID ANRIAS

*With numerous illustrations
of Zodiacal Types
By the Author*

ASTROLOGY CLASSICS
Maryland

On the cover: The crowd outside the London Science Museum, South Kensington, 1980. Photo by David R. Roell.

The publisher wishes to thank Dr. H. of Regulus Astrology LLC, for bringing this book to his attention.

ISBN: 978 1 933303 40 6

Man and the Zodiac was first published in 1938.
This edition, 2010

Published by
Astrology Classics
the publication division of
The Astrology Center of America
207 Victory Lane, Bel Air MD 21014
on line at www.**AstroAmerica.com**

INTRODUCTION TO THE SECOND EDITION

David Anrias, a sensitive who was taught by the Masters, exceeds in Astrology and Art. This gifted man has given us methods for synchronizing the planets, the houses and their mutual aspects in order to delineate nativities. Even with no previous knowledge of astrology, it is possible to use this method advantageously.

This ingenious author has not only lucidly described the signs and their decadents, but his facile pen has actually pictured them. Since they are clothed in 1938 styles, today's readers may find it difficult to picture their friends and relatives in the illustrations. However, the illustrations have been left as they were produced at the time of the book's publication. If the imagination is used to reclothe the figures in today's fashion, it will be found they are no longer strange. In truth, Scorpio will not need reclothing!

David Anrias points out that it is Exoteric Astrology, which clearly outlines the relation of the Zodiac to the human body; and the planets, themselves, in relation to the body defines the affinity between them and the signs.

By his placement of the planets, he has found an easy way of calculating aspects. In achieving this he set before the reader, the influence of the luminaries and the planets. On the subject of luminaries, he considers them in relation to the elements—fiery signs, airy signs, watery signs and earthy signs. He has been thorough in his delineations.

Perhaps one of the most interesting subjects in relation to the person, himself, is the knowledge of the diseases to which the signs are subject. In this category, he has touched on that most important aspect of daily life—diet.

Esoteric Astrology delves into the twelve signs of the Zodiac in relation to the three Minds—conscious, unconscious and superconscious. As man ascends into more enlightened levels, he will want to analyze all the aspects of The Esoteric field.

David Anrias includes two nativities — Wagner's and the Duchess of Windsor's. For the beginner and the advanced student, they will be most instructive.

Sibyl Ferguson

January 15, 1970

CONTENTS

		PAGE
FOREWORD	. . . .	xiii

BOOK I

EXOTERIC ASTROLOGY

CHAP.

I   A BRIEF DEFINITION OF ASTROLOGY . . 3
    The Solar System—The Constellations—The Planets.

II THE TWELVE HOUSES OF THE HOROSCOPE . 7
    The Twelve Houses related to the Twelve Signs—The Four Elements—The Constitutions—The Zodiac in relation to the Human Body—The Planets in relation to the Body—Affinity between Signs and Planets.

III HOW TO FIND THE RISING SIGN . . . 18
    Placing the Planets—The Aspects—An Easy Way of calculating Aspects.

IV THE INFLUENCE OF THE LUMINARIES AND THE PLANETS 28
    The Sun—The Moon—Mercury—Venus—Mars—Jupiter—Saturn—Uranus—Neptune.

V   THE ASPECTS. 38
    Conjunctions—Adverse Aspects—Benefic Aspects.

VI THE LUMINARIES IN RELATION TO THE SIGNS . 52
    The Signs considered as Elements—Fiery Signs—Airy Signs—Watery Signs—Earthy Signs—The Diseases to which each Rising Sign is subject—Rising Planets—The Decanates.

CONTENTS

CHAP.		PAGE
VII	THE TWELVE RISING SIGNS AND THEIR DECANATE INFLUENCES	64
	The appearance of each Decanate—The changing age from Pisces to Aquarius.	
VIII	THE INFLUENCE OF PLANETS IN HOUSES. .	114
IX	HEALTH AND THE HYLEG	137
	Healing and the New Age—Cures effected through diet.	
X	TRANSITS	143
	The Progressed Horoscope—Eclipses.	
XI	THE ART OF SYNTHESIS	152
	Some opposing and complementary Houses—The Mind and the Emotions.	
XII	WAGNER'S NATIVITY	165
	A Brief Delineation—Mundane and Psychological effects of Retrograde Planets.	

BOOK II

ESOTERIC ASTROLOGY

I	AN EASTERN SUBJECTIVE METHOD APPLIED TO AN ASTROLOGICAL PROBLEM . . .	177
II	THE TWELVE SIGNS OF THE ZODIAC IN RELATION TO THE CONSCIOUS, UNCONSCIOUS AND SUPERCONSCIOUS MINDS	181
	The Nativities of Napoleon I, Hitler and Mussolini in relation to their National Unconscious—The Four Final Signs in relation to the Superconscious mind and the Coming Age.	

APPENDIX

AN AMERICAN NATIVITY—THE HOROSCOPE OF THE DUCHESS OF WINDSOR . . . 199

SOME FURTHER NOTES ON SETTING UP A CHART 203

INDEX 207

ILLUSTRATIONS

The Twelve Signs of the Zodiac . *Frontispiece*

	PAGE
The Zodiac in Relation to the Human Body	13

The Decanate Influences:

1. Leo Decanate of Aries 68
2. Sagittarius Decanate of Aries. . . 68
3. Virgo Decanate of Taurus . . . 71
4. Capricorn Decanate of Taurus . . 71
5. Libra Decanate of Gemini . . . 75
6. Aquarius Decanate of Gemini . . . 75
7. Scorpio Decanate of Cancer . . . 77
8. Pisces Decanate of Cancer . . . 77
9. Sagittarius Decanate of Leo . . . 81
10. Aries Decanate of Leo 81
11. Capricorn Decanate of Virgo . . . 85
12. Taurus Decanate of Virgo . . . 85
13. Aquarius Decanate of Libra . . . 87
14. Gemini Decanate of Libra . . . 87
15. Pisces-Cancer combination of Scorpio, 19 degrees Rising 91
16. Sagittarius Decanate of Sagittarius. . 95
17. Aries Decanate of Sagittarius. . . 95
18. Leo Decanate of Sagittarius . . . 95
19. Taurus Decanate of Capricorn . . 99
20. Virgo Decanate of Capricorn . . . 99

ILLUSTRATIONS

THE DECANATE INFLUENCES—*continued* PAGE
21. GEMINI DECANATE OF AQUARIUS . . . 103
22. LIBRA DECANATE OF AQUARIUS . . . 103
23. CANCER-SCORPIO COMBINATION OF PISCES, 19 DEGREES RISING 109
24. A LIBRA-GEMINI TYPE, 28 DEGREES RISING, DRAWN FROM LIFE 113

CHARTS

	PAGE
THE TWELVE HOUSES	8
NOON, LONDON, 21ST MARCH, 1937	22
WAGNER'S NATIVITY	166
MUSSOLINI'S NATIVITY	188
HITLER'S NATIVITY	191
THE DUCHESS OF WINDSOR'S NATIVITY . . .	199

The sketch marked No. 24 is the only portrait. The others are Zodiacal types resembling many Europeans born under the same ascendant or decanate influence.

FOREWORD

FROM the dawn of history the signs of the Zodiac have been depicted upon innumerable temples and churches in every land. Civilizations have waxed and waned, but the signs of the Zodiac, being based upon fundamental principles, have continued to influence mankind. For this reason the twelve signs and their decanate types have been illustrated in detail in this book. These sketches are the result of many years' astrological study and also artistic observation from known birth data.[1] If this book proves helpful for the beginner to recognize the various rising signs and their respective decanates it will have achieved its purpose.

The chapter on the Art of Synthesis contains a method of synchronizing the planets, houses and their mutual aspects which has proved helpful in delineating numerous nativities for those who had had no previous knowledge of astrology. In the

---

[1] These drawings are typical of the decanate types only. The appearance can be modified by rising planets, the luminaries' position or that of the ruling planet.

FOREWORD

final chapter " the unconscious " is co-related to certain signs of the Zodiac and is supported by three nativities to reinforce my contention. This idea was originally derived from one sentence in an old Indian treatise and later elaborated in my own books. The chapter connecting the conscious and superconscious minds with the remaining signs has been conceived through the Eastern subjective method described in Chapter I (Book II).

My appreciative thanks are due to Mrs. Ralph Gell for her charming wrapper design of the Zodiac in relation to her son's nativity ; to Miss Ursula Greville for permission to reprint the frontispiece and Wagner's nativity from her magazine, *The Sackbut*; to Mr. F. B. Marsom for several apposite suggestions, and finally to Miss Foll and Miss Fuller who proved very helpful regarding the main essentials of what purports to be but a simple outline of a vast thesis.

DAVID ANRIAS.

WESTWARD HO ! DEVON,
September, 1937.

BOOK I
EXOTERIC ASTROLOGY

The decanates of the Zodiac

Sign	0-10°	10-20°	20-30°
Aries	Aries	Leo	Sagittarius
Taurus	Taurus	Virgo	Capricorn
Gemini	Gemini	Libra	Aquarius
Cancer	Cancer	Scorpio	Pisces
Leo	Leo	Sagittarius	Aries
Virgo	Virgo	Capricorn	Taurus
Libra	Libra	Aquarius	Gemini
Scorpio	Scorpio	Pisces	Cancer
Sagittarius	Sagittarius	Aries	Leo
Capricorn	Capricorn	Taurus	Virgo
Aquarius	Aquarius	Gemini	Libra
Pisces	Pisces	Cancer	Scorpio

Publisher's note: The Anrias rulerships are not the same as in most other sources. If your ascendant is exactly 10 or 20°, pick the delineation that best suits.

CHAPTER I

A BRIEF DEFINITION OF ASTROLOGY

ASTROLOGY is a word derived from the Greek *astron*, star, and *logos*, science. It has been called the soul of Astronomy and gave birth to that science, for the origin of astrology is lost in antiquity. The modern astronomer observes in detail the outward activities of the stars and their courses. The astrologer seeks to realize and then establish a connexion between the changing aspects of the stars and the varying course of human life, and thence to predict events or to suggest the best way to achieve desired ends subject to the limitations of each nativity.

Astronomers seek to acquire knowledge of the objective manifestations of the stellar heavens. Astrologers confine their attention to the subjective side of the same laws and endeavour to apply their knowledge to the character and destiny of man in his relation to fundamental principles. Thus the main objective of astrology is the study of man in order that he may know himself. In other words, each student of astrology becomes

EXOTERIC ASTROLOGY

aware of his weaknesses and frustrations as expressed through malefic influences, and realizes his inner integrity and mundane possibilities as revealed through his benefic planets and aspects.

THE SOLAR SYSTEM

The Sun is the centre of our system. Our earth is one of the bodies circling round it, performing one revolution in one year of $365\frac{1}{4}$ days.

The earth revolves round the Sun in an elliptical orbit, whose plane, named the ecliptic, makes an angle of $23\frac{1}{2}$ degrees with the plane of the equator. The plane of the equator continued indefinitely to reach the celestial sphere marks out the celestial equator, and it is the belt extending $23\frac{1}{2}$ degrees on each side of this which is named the Zodiac. The planets revolve round the Sun in varying distances from it and the planes of their orbits are inclined at various angles to the plane of the equator, but the orbits all lie so that the planets revolve within the above-named belt, i.e. the Zodiac.

The constellations which lie within this belt are the well-known signs of the Zodiac. These are:

♈ Aries, the Ram.   ♌ Leo, the Lion.
♉ Taurus, the Bull.   ♍ Virgo, the Virgin.
♊ Gemini, the Twins.   ♎ Libra, the Scales.
♋ Cancer, the Crab.   ♏ Scorpio, the Scorpion.

A BRIEF DEFINITION OF ASTROLOGY

♐ Sagittarius, the Archer.
♒ Aquarius, the Waterbearer.
♑ Capricorn, the Goat.
♓ Pisces, the Fishes.

By a process of visualization the symbols soon become memorized in connexion with their names if taken in the above order.

The earth as it rotates upon its axis from West to East, witnesses the phenomena of the luminaries, the various planets and the fixed stars traversing the heavens, by rising, culminating and setting, whilst the earth appears to remain stationary.

The Sun seems to revolve round the earth once in 24 hours, but this is an illusion, caused by the earth's rotation. Yet the Sun is actually moving through space with his planets towards a point in the constellation Hercules. This book is only concerned with the effects of the luminaries and seven planets upon man in a psychological and physical sense.

Taken in order from the Sun as they revolve round it, Mercury is the nearest planet, then Venus, the Earth, Mars, Jupiter, Saturn, Uranus, Neptune, and Pluto. Of the last planet's characteristics so little is known at present that it will not be considered as an astrological influence in this book,[1] which is only a brief outline of certain

[1] My comments regarding Pluto in my last year's *Ephemeris* has aroused much controversy. Pluto was only discovered in 1930 and it is therefore much too early to allow oneself

EXOTERIC ASTROLOGY

astrological traditions, combined with a few ideas which are applied to the present condition of world changes.

The symbols of the planets are as follows:

☉ The Sun; ☽ The Moon; ☿ Mercury; ♀ Venus; ⊕ Earth; ♂ Mars; ♃ Jupiter; ♄ Saturn; ♅ Uranus; ♆ Neptune; ♇ Pluto.

to form fixed and conclusive opinions upon this orb in any final manner. . . .
We must confess to a very marked prejudice against "Pluto" because he invariably comes up associated with underworld activities and curious affairs of violence.
At the time of the Great War in 1914 Pluto was on the Summer Solstice (0°♋), conjunct of Saturn.

A very significant feature of people born under the ray of the outside orbs (Uranus and Neptune) is that they are always "strangers" upon the world, but not of it, aloof—the odd one of the family.—" Debatable Points ", Raphael's *Ephemeris*, 1934.

The voice of the collective, in so far as it acts upon individuals, is symbolized by the trinity of remote planets: Uranus, Neptune and Pluto. It is significant that these have become publicly known at a time when humanity is breaking through isolating barriers of creeds and dogmas, and materially if not yet spiritually, all men flow into the ocean of a common humanity.—*The Astrology of Personality*, by Dane Rudhyar.

CHAPTER II

THE TWELVE HOUSES OF THE HOROSCOPE

ASSUMING that the earth is the centre to be considered, it is not difficult to visualize the Sun rising at daybreak on the Eastern horizon, thereby forming the ascendant. At noon the Sun reaches the Meridian, called the mid-heaven; at Sunset it is in the vicinity of seventh house and at midnight in the neighbourhood of the fourth house cusp. These four important positions are called cardinal points or "Angles". The arbitrary diagram created for casting a horoscope is a wheel or circle consisting of twelve "spokes" dividing one house from the next. The first house includes the space between the cusp of the ascendant and the cusp of the second house.[1] A planet placed within a few degrees either side of any cusp influences the two houses each side of it.

The first, fourth, seventh, and tenth houses are called *Angular*. Those that come next, the second, fifth, eighth, and eleventh, are called *Succedent*.

[1] These proceed from the left below the horizon in anti-clockwise order.

THE TWELVE HOUSES

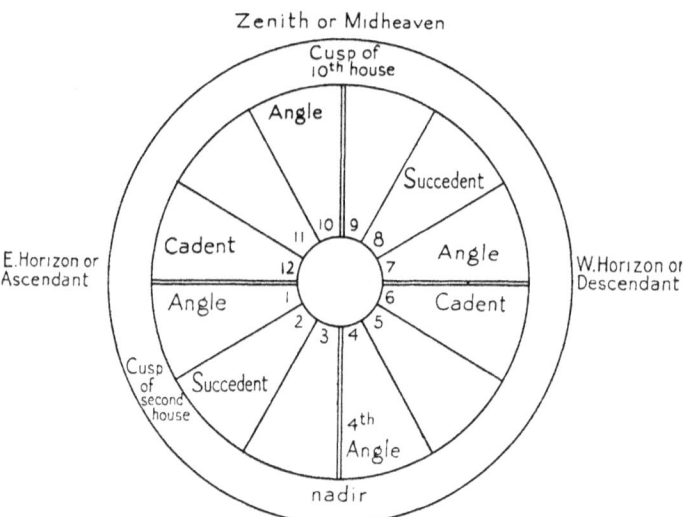

A chart or horoscope consists of 12 segments of a circle equally divided up into 12 houses.

THE TWELVE HOUSES OF THE HOROSCOPE

The remaining four, the third, sixth, ninth, and twelfth, are the *Cadent* houses, called so because they fall away from the Angles, as the ninth falls away from the tenth cusp for example.

To stress the importance of the Angles as such, a double line is frequently put within the wheel or circle, thereby forming a cross. The circle itself is divided into 360 degrees. Within this area all the aspects that make up a nativity are formed.

THE TWELVE HOUSES TAKE ON THE QUALITIES OF THE TWELVE SIGNS

Both the houses and the signs possess the same characteristics at one and the same time when the first degrees of Aries are rising upon the ascendant.

According to astrological tradition, the twelve houses and their characteristics took on the qualities of the twelve signs.

The first house was likened to the fiery sign Aries, and so was co-related to the physical body and its varying capacity for action.

The second house became associated with the earthy fixed sign Taurus, which gave of the fruits of the earth and so was known as the house of finance.

The third house, being compared to that of Gemini, the twins, concerned brethren, and through its airy mental quality became expressed through writing, travelling and rapid transit of thought or action.

The fourth house assumed the watery maternal influence of the sign Cancer, under the rule of the Moon, and so dealt with the home and the parents' affairs, also the end of life.

The fifth house was concerned with desire and its fruits, viz. children, through the passionate fiery sign Leo. The drama and other ventures were also associated with this house.

The sixth house dealt with work, service and sickness and defined the earthy limitations of the sign Virgo.

The seventh house expressed poise and balance and so was connected with partnerships and likened to Libra, the airy sign of the scales.

The eighth house revealed the possibilities of death or regeneration through the watery fixed sign Scorpio.

The ninth house, through its spiritual quality, gave the power to acquire the fiery intuition of Sagittarius, the archer, sending his shafts of thought towards heaven.

The tenth house took on the earthy active quality of the sign Capricorn, which is chiefly concerned with attaining recognition, power and worldly success.

The eleventh house became associated with the

THE TWELVE HOUSES OF THE HOROSCOPE

ability to co-operate with others through the airy mental power of the sign Aquarius.

The twelfth house expressed either the desired introspection of the hermit or the unwilling confinement of the prisoner. Pisces, being a dual watery sign, contained both these possibilities within its influence.

THE FOUR ELEMENTS

The twelve signs considered above were divided into four elements : Fire ; Air ; Water ; Earth. These respectively corresponded to the spirit, mind, soul and body of man, symbolizing his spiritual, mental, psychic and physical states of consciousness. The signs were distributed as follows :

FIRE	EARTH	AIR	WATER
1 Aries	2 Taurus	3 Gemini	4 Cancer
5 Leo	6 Virgo	7 Libra	8 Scorpio
9 Sagittarius	10 Capricorn	11 Aquarius	12 Pisces

THE CONSTITUTIONS

Each of the signs is either active, fixed or mutable. The " cardinal " are active or restless ; the " fixed " positive or determined ; the mutable could alternate between the two, sometimes one, sometimes the other. The signs are qualified thus :

EXOTERIC ASTROLOGY

ACTIVE	FIXED	MUTABLE
1 Aries	2 Taurus	3 Gemini
4 Cancer	5 Leo	6 Virgo
7 Libra	8 Scorpio	9 Sagittarius
10 Capricorn	11 Aquarius	12 Pisces

FURTHER CLASSIFICATIONS

The odd signs, Aries, Gemini, etc., are masculine; the even signs, Taurus, Cancer, etc., are feminine.

The human signs are Gemini, Virgo, Aquarius and the last half of Sagittarius. The sign Libra, added to the Zodiac by the Greeks, is also human.

The animal signs are Aries, Taurus, Leo and Capricorn, representing the ram, the bull, the lion and the goat.

Double signs symbolize two children, the centaur and two fishes through Gemini, Sagittarius and Pisces respectively.

The fruitful signs are Taurus, Cancer, Scorpio, Sagittarius and Pisces; the sterile signs are Aries, Gemini, Leo, Libra; Capricorn and Aquarius can be either.

THE ZODIAC IN RELATION TO THE HUMAN BODY

The twelve signs of the Zodiac and the planets ruling them are related to various parts of the body. Reference to the accompanying diagram will show their connexion.

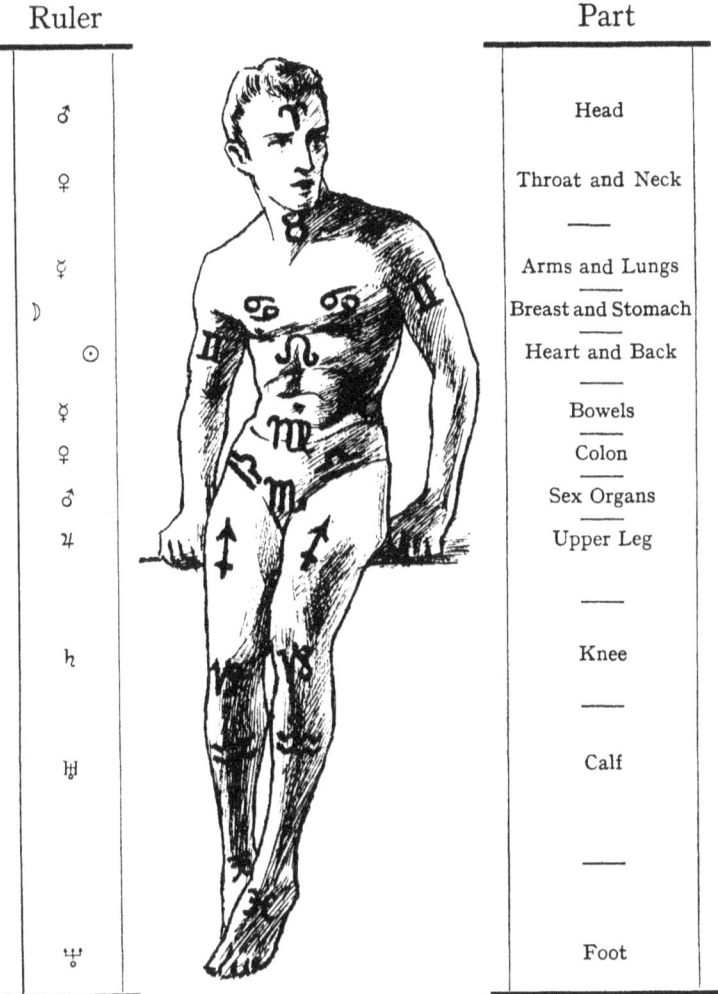

EXOTERIC ASTROLOGY

With regard to the internal organs, the signs are thus distributed: Aries, the brain; Cancer, the digestion; Libra, the kidneys; Capricorn, the spleen; Leo, the heart; Scorpio, the generative system; Aquarius, the nervous system; Gemini, the lungs; Virgo, the bowels. The other signs have less influence in a direct sense over the internal organs.

THE PLANETS WITH RELATION TO THE BODY

Neptune has sway over the sympathetic system, and when upon the ascendant there is frequently the latent power to practise psychometry or telepathy if reinforced elsewhere in the nativity.

Uranus governs the nervous system, which is closely related to the brain in advanced types and under the control of the will.

Saturn rules the spleen, the liver and the bony structure. It is a masculine or hermaphrodite planet according to the *Brihat Jataka*, an Indian fifth-century astrological book.

Mars controls the muscles, the sinews and the sex organs. It rules the *internal* generative system in women.

Venus governs the throat, reins, ovaries and the *internal* generative system in men.

Mercury governs the lungs and the nervous system. The bowels can be controlled through the influence of this planet by certain schools of

THE TWELVE HOUSES OF THE HOROSCOPE

Indian magic. It is a feminine or hermaphrodite planet according to the *Brihat Jataka* of Varaha Mihira. The Indians assert that the positive and negative forces of the human body can be controlled by a neutral third connected with the spinal cord through the influence of this planet, hence the stressing of the latent hermaphrodite trait within it.

The *Moon* rules the upper stomach (as opposed to Mercury, ruling the bowels) and also the lymphatic system. It is a negative influence especially if ruling the ascendant.

Certain planets have greater affinity and power when placed in particular signs. When this fortunate combination takes place the planet is said to be " exalted ". The same planet placed in the opposite sign is considered weak and said to be in its " fall ". Similarly planets are said to be " detriment " when placed in the opposite signs to those under their rulership.

AFFINITY BETWEEN SIGNS AND PLANETS, ALSO THE REVERSE

Saturn is exalted in Libra in its fall in Aries.
Jupiter	,,	in Cancer	,,	in Capricorn.
Mars	,,	in Capricorn	,,	in Cancer.
Sun	,,	in Aries	,,	in Libra.
Venus	,,	in Pisces	,,	in Virgo.
Mercury	,,	in Virgo	,,	in Pisces.
Moon	,,	in Taurus	,,	in Scorpio.

EXOTERIC ASTROLOGY

Just as a student of chemistry accepts what is told him in his early efforts in the laboratory, so too must the astrological student accept the first elements of this science if he would acquire any knowledge or intuition of an individual nature. To read horoscopes correctly requires, like everything else, *practice* and not a little discrimination. Gradually the potential astrologer will acquire the power to differentiate, according to the combination of planets, signs and houses, the subjective type of man from one who is only interested in objective or mundane matters. He will soon realize that he who is difficult to influence has several planets in fixed signs : he who has much enthusiasm is dominated by the cardinal or active elements. Whilst he who is indecisive usually has an undesirable combination of mutable influences. Similarly fiery signs predominating in a chart indicate an energetic nature ; earthy ones a practical disposition ; airy signs that of the scientist or mental idealist ; whilst watery signs open the door to the world of sensation. A well-poised nature usually implies an equal distribution of planets in signs and elements. An unbalanced nature, however, would have afflicted planets congested in one element or another.

Put briefly, a horoscope may be compared to a musical symphony, with all the combinations of harmony and discord, peace and restlessness that

THE TWELVE HOUSES OF THE HOROSCOPE

such implies. An experienced astrologer might equally be likened to a trained musician, capable of comprehending each subtle nuance of a composition ; nuances that would remain unrealized by the lay mind.

CHAPTER III

HOW TO FIND THE RISING SIGN AND PLACE THE PLANETS

TO find the ascendant or rising sign and to set up a chart, an ephemeris is needed showing the daily positions of the planets throughout the particular year and the zodiacal positions at every time of the day. Raphael's *Ephemerides* are published for 1s. each for any year as far back as 1850, and can be obtained from W. Foulsham & Co., Red Lion Court, London, E.C.4.

For the beginner it is proposed to give, without elaboration, the essential rules which will enable the chart for a birth at any place within the British Isles to be set up in a few minutes, and with sufficient accuracy for a delineation on the lines suggested in these pages. The additional rules necessary for drawing a chart for any place in the world, and with meticulous accuracy, are given in the Appendix.

The position of the Zodiacal signs on the cusps of the houses is entirely dependent on the *time* of birth, and it is necessary to ascertain this with the

HOW TO FIND THE RISING SIGN

greatest possible accuracy. If the birth took place in the summer months, it can be assumed that *Summer* Time has been given, and this must be converted to Greenwich Time by the subtraction of one hour.

It is important to remember that the *Ephemeris* gives the *Noon* positions of the planets.

The drawing up of a chart falls into two stages : the first, the placing of the Zodiacal signs on the cusps of the houses, for which purpose *Sidereal* Time is used : the second, the placing of the planets in their correct Zodiacal degrees, for which purpose *Greenwich* Time is used. *This distinction must be borne in mind.*

For the beginner it is as well to choose as simple a figure as possible, so the horoscope is selected for Noon in London on the 21st March, 1937. All that is required is an ephemeris for that year, and a blank diagram as shown on page 8.

For the first stage we turn to the monthly table for March, and note the Sidereal Time given in the second column against the chosen date, 23 hr. 54 min. We then turn to the " Table of Houses for London " at the back of the *Ephemeris*, and run the eye down the left-hand column of each table until we find the closest approximation to the Sidereal Time, 23 hr. 56 min. The remaining figures on this line give the Zodiacal degrees on the cusps of the tenth, eleventh, twelfth, first (or

EXOTERIC ASTROLOGY

ascendant), second, and third houses as follows: ♓ 29 : ♉ 8 : ♊ 21 : ♋ 26 : ♌ 12 : ♍ 3. It is important to note that although a sign is shown at the top of each column, this sometimes changes half-way down. After taking down the number it is therefore necessary to run the eye *up* the column, and to take down the first sign shown. In the present case, for example, the sign on the eleventh cusp is ♉ and not ♈.

We then enter these figures and signs against the correct houses in the blank form, and put down the *same* figures on the opposite cusps, adding the symbols of the opposite signs, thus ♑ 26 opposite the Ascendant, and ♍ 29 opposite the tenth house. When this has been done, we observe that the signs of Virgo and Pisces are repeated on successive cusps, whilst Aries and Leo do not appear. In such a case the missing signs are known as " Intercepted "[1] and should be put in the chart in their correct position in the order of the signs, but without any figure for degrees as the whole of the intercepted sign naturally falls in the one house.

(For any time other than noon, it would have been necessary to adjust the Sidereal Time, adding time elapsed *after* noon, or deducting time *until*

---

[1] The " Interception " of a sign is due to the fact that the Zodiac is oblique to the earth and so appears to be pulled out in some places and squeezed together into a smaller compass in others.

HOW TO FIND THE RISING SIGN

noon. If the birth had been at 3 p.m. the Sidereal Time would have been 23 hr. 54 min. plus three hours; the result exceeds 24 hours, so 24 hours is deducted, giving a time of 2 hr. 54 min. and an Ascendant of ♌ 27. If the birth had been at 3 a.m., nine hours would be deducted, giving a time of 14 hr. 54 min. and an Ascendant of ♑ 10. If the Sidereal Time is too small to permit a deduction, twenty-four hours should be added first.)

PLACING THE PLANETS

For the second stage we turn back to the monthly table to extract the Zodiacal positions of the planets, which appear under the columns headed by the symbols and the word "Long". For the 21st March, 1937, these are as follows:

Sun	♈ ½	Saturn	♓ 26
Moon	♋ 26	Jupiter	♑ 23
Neptune	♍ 17	Mars	♐ 2
Uranus	♉ 7	Venus	♉ 5
	Mercury	♓ 27	

As the chart is being drawn for noon, whilst the *ephemeris* is calculated for noon, the above positions are accurate. The planets' movement in the course of the day is so small that for the present purpose they can be disregarded, with the one exception of the *Moon*. The latter moves

21st March, 1937. Noon, London. Sidereal Time at Noon 23 hr. 54 min.

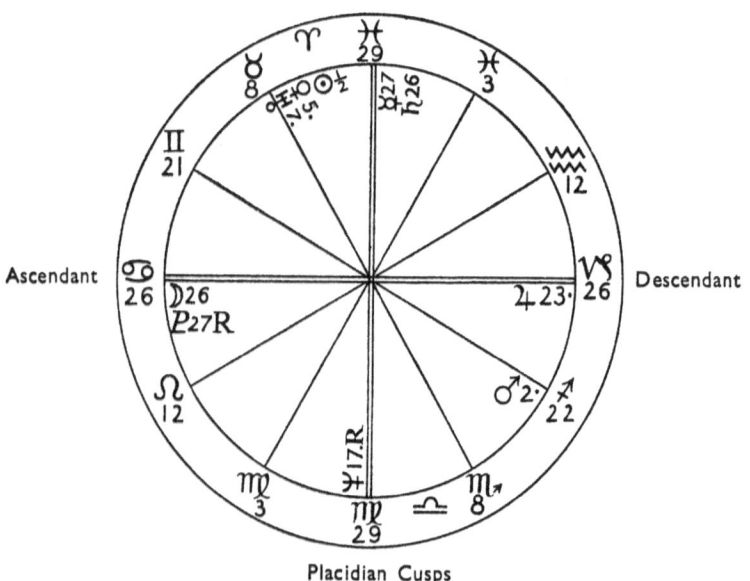

Placidian Cusps

Sun exalted
Moon in it's own sign
Venus "   "   "
Mercury in it's fall
Jupitor "   "   "

4 earth
4 water
0 air
2 fire
4 mutable
4 cardinal
2 fixed

HOW TO FIND THE RISING SIGN

approximately thirteen degrees in one day, and its position must be corrected for the number of hours before or after noon.

(The Moon's position above is ♋ 26. If the hour of birth had been 3 a.m., the Moon would have been 9/24ths short of its noon position, or say four degrees, giving a position of ♋ 22.)

The positions as extracted are now transferred to the form, and every care is taken to insert the planets on the correct side of the respective cusps. The order of the signs is *anti-clockwise* round the chart, whilst each house may contain parts of two or even three signs. The sixth house, for example, contains the twenty-first to thirtieth degrees of Sagittarius *plus* the first twenty-six degrees of Capricorn. The two degrees of Mars therefore fall in the *fifth* house, whilst the twenty-three degrees of Jupiter correctly fall in the *sixth* house. This house also provides a good example of the fact that the planets *must* be entered *near* to the cusp of their signs. ♃ 23 entered in the *middle* of the house might be in either Sagittarius or Capricorn. But noted near the sixth cusp it is clearly in the former sign, and vice versa. The figure is now finished.

As a rough check it may be remembered that the Sun's position for a noon or midnight birth is always in the vicinity of the mid-heaven or nadir respectively. It is similarly near the ascen-

EXOTERIC ASTROLOGY

dant or seventh house for births in the early morning or early evening.

THE ASPECTS

An "aspect" is the distance between any two Zodiacal positions or any two planets. They are as follows:

GOOD			BAD	
✶ Sextile	60°	☍	Opposition	180°
⚺ Semi-Sextile	30°	□	Square	90°
△ Trine	120°	∠	Semi-square	45°
⚻ Quincunx	150°	⚼	Sesqui-quadrate	135°

☌ The conjunction is sometimes good, sometimes bad. The conjunction is within eight degrees and easily seen. So are oppositions and squares, for they occur from signs of the same Quadruplicity—cardinal, fixed or mutable. Trines are formed from the same Triplicity (of fire, air, water or earth). Sextiles occur between signs with but one intervening and the lesser aspects can be ignored at the moment.

AN EASY WAY OF CALCULATING ASPECTS

Looking at the figure, it can be seen that the luminaries are in trine aspect, for the same triplicity or watery element is involved. The aspect is only four degrees apart. Each planet has an orb or "sphere" of influence, which extends into

HOW TO FIND THE RISING SIGN

space and becomes the "aura" of the planet. The orbs are as follows:

For conjunction or opposition allow eight degrees when the Sun aspects the Moon, and a degree less when either luminary aspects a planet, or for planets aspecting each other. Allow about eight degrees all round for square or trine. For sextile about six degrees. For semi-square and sesquidrate, about three degrees, for semi-sextile and quincunx two degrees.

In this case it is easy to see that both Saturn and Mercury are in conjunction with the Sun. If we look at the Sun and Mars, it can be seen that Mars has twenty-eight degrees of Sagittarius, thirty degrees of Capricorn, thirty degrees of Aquarius and thirty degrees of Pisces to reach the Sun's position, making 118 degrees in all. This aspect is within three degrees of a trine, although formed from different elements. Similarly Mercury has three degrees of Pisces, thirty degrees of Aries, thirty degrees of Taurus, thirty degrees of Gemini and twenty-six degrees of Cancer—moving anti-clockwise—to reach the Moon's position. Added, these figures make the trine aspect 119 degrees. When calculating this way, the intercepted signs must not be forgotten nor the fact that both Virgo and Pisces influence four houses. An intercepted sign is frequently as powerful as a planet.

EXOTERIC ASTROLOGY

Work downwards: Sun to Moon; Moon to Mercury, etc. It simplifies matters not to put down the same aspect twice such as Moon to Mercury and again Mercury to Moon. This method prevents redundancy.

When an aspect is completed, the swifter influence is then *separating* from the other. *Application*, however, is the motion of the swifter body gaining upon the other, about to form an aspect which is not yet exact.

Planets are in *mutual reception* if in each other's signs, such as Saturn in Cancer and the Moon in Capricorn. But if considered singly they are both in *detriment*. A planet is void of course if it forms no complete aspect before entering another sign.

Unfortunately many people do not know the exact time at which they were born. There is one method of obtaining the time of birth called rectification, involving the pre-natal epoch, but this procedure is beyond the powers of the elementary student.

On the other hand, many people show marked Zodiacal and planetary characteristics, which can be successfully intuited by observant people interested in physiognomy. For their benefit twenty-four variations of Zodiacal types are included in this book.

The usual astrological tradition has been followed here in calling some aspects " good " and

HOW TO FIND THE RISING SIGN

others " bad ". Each nativity contains various potentialities. The " good " aspects promise physical benefits or mental ability which are easily realized, whilst " bad " aspects indicate latent strength, to be acquired only after an intense struggle. In terms of practical psychology or constructive thought it would be better to regard these aspects as " harmonious " or " strenuous " influences.

CHAPTER IV

THE INFLUENCE OF THE LUMINARIES AND THE PLANETS

THE SUN

THE Sun is but a small part of the limitless whole, yet to the astrologer it is the Divine Being, the Solar Logos, the source of energy and life for our particular system. In a nativity it is associated with man's individual or subjective essence, which will be coloured by the characteristics of the sign the Sun was placed in at birth. It is a giver of life, but is so impersonal in its influence that the average man rarely contacts its higher qualities in a conscious or positive sense. When well placed by sign and house it gives power, authority, will and self-reliance. In the body it corresponds to the heart, and with regard to the signs, it is associated with those that are fixed. If the Sun be afflicted at birth by the Moon or the ascendant, the vitality will be feeble in an objective sense and the will-power weak in a subjective way. If the Sun has no aspects at all, the person concerned is hardly touched by its in-

INFLUENCE OF THE LUMINARIES

fluence. This fact should be taken into consideration with regard to those general prophecies—made only in connexion with the Sun's position—by the weekly press, for so much depends upon its aspects or house position regarding its influence.

THE MOON

The Moon moves in a plane inclined to the ecliptic about five degrees and cutting it at two points. These points are called the ☊ Dragon's Head [1] and Dragon's Tail ☋. The Head and Tail are the North and South nodes and make a complete circuit of the ecliptic in about nineteen years, thereby causing eclipses to occur. A Solar eclipse can be very important if it fall adversely upon any critical point or conjunction in a nativity. This event sometimes causes death and is caused by the Moon passing between the earth and the Sun, taking place at New Moon. Lunar eclipses take place at Full Moon and are caused by the earth passing between the Sun and the Moon. These are not considered so drastic as the former unless they afflict some critical point in the nativity.

The Moon is associated with the feelings and

---

[1] The dragon's head is the North node and considered good. The dragon's tail is the South node and considered evil. Unless in conjunction with any planet or critical point, they are not considered very important.

EXOTERIC ASTROLOGY

with sensation. According to Indian astrology, it stands for the temporary reincarnating personality. If in the mid-heaven it is not too much to say it dominates the whole horoscope, subjectively and objectively. The personality will be well in evidence and demanding all that it can out of life, both physically and emotionally. Should the Moon be rising in the first house, it is almost as strong in effecting the outlook and desires as if in the mid-heaven. The whole temperament will desire public recognition and be subject to the sway of the particular mood of the moment.

MERCURY

Called " the winged Messenger of the Gods " by the Greeks, is the planet nearest the Sun, and is considered convertible by the astrologer, neither positive nor negative, but capable of being both when represented in its highest individualized influence as the Thinker. It governs the sense of *seeing* and also the mind, both in an objective and subjective sense. In every nativity it represents the ego in physical manifestation. At the close of the life it signifies the wisdom or knowledge acquired. In the advanced man it is the higher subjective mind, free from desire, manipulating the negative and positive currents of force (associated with *Venus* and *Mars*) represented as circulating on each side of a neutral third connected

INFLUENCE OF THE LUMINARIES

with the spinal column. The Caduceus thus becomes a winged rod, round which two serpents are entwined.[1] Polarized between the *impersonal* life of the *Sun* and the higher and lower emotions associated with *Venus* and *Mars*, *Mercury* became in *past* cycles self-conscious force in the Adept. In the case of the advanced man it frees the mind from desire, through a process of detached analysis, especially if these three planets are in conjunction in a mental or subjective house. In this way the position of *Mercury* and its aspects has far more importance than that of the *Sun*, a fact which is not sufficiently stressed in Modern Astrology.

VENUS

Venus is associated with the emotions or aspirations that arise from *within* the man as opposed to those stimulated from without (under *Mars*). Thus she rules the higher side of the nature, making for harmony, friendship and soul union in the highest sense, thereby tending to become unselfish. As a central force *within man* she stands for the human soul or higher subjective mind polarized *within* the heart.[2] As an *external* force

---

[1] The two serpents here being symbolical of the mental and emotional desires.

[2] This central force has been the source of life for the Adept and is correlated to the planet Venus, whose human evolution

operating *through women* she becomes the physical embodiment of beauty inspiring artists and poets or influencing men especially associated with Venusian occupations, such as stage managers, musical directors, dressmakers, florists, etc.

MARS

In evolved *women Mars* is associated with the *internal* fire of selfless devotion to a cause, where personal desires are sacrificed to some inner urge for service, as in the case of Florence Nightingale.[1] Then the internal fire, vitalizing the sympathetic system, is raised upward to the head centre. In lesser types this force is expressed either as personal ambition or else as the desire to attract and

is far in advance of our own, and now approaching its inevitable apotheosis. Therefore this occult force is becoming too rarefied and *introverted* to be used as an *external* spiritual stimulus to our own evolution. Thus an occult metamorphosis *both* in the Adept and in the advanced man is even now taking place: attuned to the mysterious sign Aquarius and the coming Age. In any case the Aquarian forces will cause a repolarization within both sexes; for Uranus influences the minds of men and the emotions of women, whilst Neptune sways the minds of women and the emotions of men. Thus the old occult method of neutralizing the forces of Mars through those of Venus is rapidly becoming abortive and will be completely obsolete before the end of this century.

[1] H. P. Blavatsky and Annie Besant also responded to this internal fire. But in the case of H. P. B. the fire became introverted, through Leo self-conscious control of Kundalini resulting in clairvoyance; whilst Annie Besant unconsciously dispersed the fire, through numerous Aries activities, and thereby closed the passing Pisces dispensation.

INFLUENCE OF THE LUMINARIES

dominate men. In *man Mars* is expressed as an *external* force and gives a fine muscular system, capable of great activity and endurance. The spirit is fearless and enterprising in advanced types. In low types the force becomes violence, lust, cruelty or abuse of power in high places.

JUPITER

Jupiter gives good fortune associated with forms and ceremonies in a mundane sense. Judges and others who dispense justice with mercy are said to come under this planet. It brings harmonious conditions when favourably placed and dignity into the life along conventional lines. In a higher sense it gives the inspired intuition which carries the mind beyond all forms into the spiritual world which has no limits, but this planet must be placed in fiery signs and in mental houses to realize such possibilities. The evils of an afflicted Jupiter on the form side become expressed through hypocrisy and sycophancy. On the life side the power of this planet is often expressed—through the fiery sign Sagittarius, and if afflicted—as reckless rebellion against law and order, combined with a general restlessness without a definite goal or objective.

EXOTERIC ASTROLOGY

SATURN

Saturn, according to Indian astrology, develops self-consciousness in the earlier stages of evolution and past births upon this planet. Later on, outgoing desires are deliberately restrained by the will. The soul learns through many lives that the aftermath of crude desires is future limitations and suffering in following incarnations. Thus prudence, refinement and endurance are acquired, and become expressed in the outer world as justice and patience. In the unevolved types the vibrations of Saturn become perverted into expressions of miserliness, envy, covetousness and cruelty. In an occult sense Saturn formed the encircling limit of consciousness until the influence of Uranus and Neptune re-polarized the subjective element of the advanced types of humanity.

URANUS

This planet of the Coming Race will influence the higher self of the future man, from beyond the " ring-pass-not " of Saturn. Thus he will become the mental wanderer and explorer between earth and heaven, whose mind is free from all forms and conventions. Already there are numerous *Uranians*, pioneers of thought and action, living almost entirely through the nervous system. These men are beyond rules and regulations and

INFLUENCE OF THE LUMINARIES

become laws unto themselves. Hence the necessity of developing poise and self-control through Saturn before attempting to contact this marvellous influence. Sudden and unexpected events occur to Uranians, frequently involving a new life under entirely different conditions and surroundings. In a mundane sense electricians and engineers come under this planet ; in a higher sense magnetic healers and reformers of all kinds, also astrologers and occultists. In an esoteric sense Uranus stands for the new type of Adept, *responding chiefly to forces beyond our Solar system* and also to the Cosmic Rays, now being investigated by modern scientists.

All things are vitalized by polarization, all *changes* wrought by re-polarization, and these changes are established by lunar influence. Thus the reversal of the motion of a satellite, incident to the reversal of the poles of the primary to which it belongs as a part of the system, will invariably bring about *the reversal of the lines of force*. The poles of *Uranus* are in reverse to those of the other (i.e. inner) planets and thus her moons are retrograde in motion, revolving reversely to our own and other planets of this system.[1]

[1] After the January Lunation 1910, when Uranus was elevated in the tenth house in conjunction to the Sun and Moon and in opposition to Neptune, and square Mars, Saturn and Jupiter, certain Indian astrologers considered that prophecies based on the influence of the planets other than Uranus

EXOTERIC ASTROLOGY

NEPTUNE

Although the last to be discovered, this planet has had an increasing influence upon the earth, since its opposition to *Uranus* between 1905 and 1912. As their moons revolve the reverse way to the remainder of our Solar system, they have an undoubted affinity with each other, especially in a catastrophic, disintegrating sense. Yet both planets act as " Awakeners ", *Uranus* in a mental sense and *Neptune* through things of the spirit. To the advanced soul, *Neptune* brings spiritual ecstasy and unusual experiences, both in sleep and the waking state, far beyond the mental scope of the average mind. The unevolved express the opposite extreme, indulging in exceptional depravity and sexual perversions, sometimes accompanied by undesirable psychic practices. In a mundane fashion *Neptune* rules democracy, arousing both the selfless socialist, and the ruthless fanatic. Similarly all those who sway others through fictitious assertions or are dominated by an idea come under this planet. Their cycle is usually but a brief one, for the immense popu-

and Neptune were likely to be frequently nullified, owing to the increasing power of the outside planets. Since then Pluto has been discovered and probably adds to the subtle upheaval in world events caused by the above lunation. See page 6 (footnote) regarding Mr. Dane Rudhyar's ideas in connexion with the three outside planets and the unconscious mind to which he has allocated them.

INFLUENCE OF THE LUMINARIES

larity is frequently followed by flight, disgrace and opprobrium, especially when *Neptune* is afflicted at birth.[1]

[1] General Boulanger had *Neptune* in the eighth house, opposition *Jupiter*, *Lord of the mid-heaven* and in square to the *Sun*. Oscar Wilde had *Neptune* angular square *Saturn*, Lord of the *mid-heaven*.

As Neptune and Uranus have great affinity with Pisces and Aquarius respectively, they tend to nullify the influence of Jupiter and Saturn, rulers of these signs. That the outer planets have greater power than the inner at this period is proved through the present state of world chaos and upheaval, with the rejection of established laws and conventions associated with the influence of the *inner* planets.

CHAPTER V

THE ASPECTS

CONJUNCTIONS

NEPTUNE

Neptune in conjunction with—

URANUS   Interest in transcendental ideas and aspirations.
SATURN   Psychic or clairaudient powers latent in the mind.
JUPITER Strong religious feeling, vivid dream experiences.
MARS   Danger from drink, chaotic desires, clandestine interests.
SUN   Clairvoyance of a practical kind in some cases : homosexual instincts in others.
VENUS   Liability to extremes with regard to feeling leading to sexual entanglements if otherwise afflicted.
MERCURY Intuitive, visionary mind which may go to extremes to the point of hallucination.

THE ASPECTS

MOON — Open to the finer forces of nature through an active sub-conscious mind and enlightening dreams.

URANUS

Uranus in conjunction with—

SATURN — Singular mind possessing both imagination and concentration, coupled with a powerful will.

JUPITER — Original mind interested in occult subjects.

MARS — Impulsive, restless, erratic mind, possessing dangerous possibilities of going to extremes.

SUN — Powerful magnetism and an inner urge to reform existing conditions in some way.

VENUS — Peculiar desires of an experimental nature. An intuitive, artistic mind possessing dramatic ability.

MERCURY — A resourceful, inventive, metaphysical mind which is agile and changeable.

MOON — Erratic, Bohemian and roving disposition, liable to be completely dominated by the attachment of the moment. Yet the mind can make dispassionate criticisms.

EXOTERIC ASTROLOGY

SATURN

Saturn in conjunction with—

JUPITER Contemplative, penetrating, discreet mind, capable of considerable concentration.

MARS. Coercive tendencies with regard to others. When the force is turned inwards, the mind becomes penetrating and intense.

SUN Poor health, sickness caused through despondency, feeble circulation. Danger of serious failure in life.

VENUS Perverse disposition, subject to varying moods.

MERCURY Austere and apprehensive mind capable of becoming exacting or persevering according to other aspects.

MOON Gloomy lethargic mind, too much inclined to negativity.

JUPITER

Jupiter in conjunction with—

MARS Courageous, enthusiastic disposition, somewhat extravagant.

SUN Candid and generous mind, success through social connexions. If afflicted, however, there is too much love of ostentation.

THE ASPECTS

VENUS
: Elegant, harmonious nature, fortunate on the whole.

MERCURY
: Hopeful, humorous, reliable temperament, prosperous general conditions.

MOON
: Joyous, gracious, sympathetic disposition. One that is popular and fortunate.

MARS

Mars in conjunction with—

SUN
: Fearless nature, but over-assertive and reckless at times. There is considerable vitality of a feverish kind.

VENUS
: Passionate nature. A strong love of sensation is indicated if Venus is neutral, and Mars is strong by sign.

MERCURY
: Enterprising mind, inclined to exaggeration and satirical remarks. There is also considerable mental credulity.

MOON
: Rash, impulsive, restless and somewhat domineering disposition. Leading to much contention.

THE SUN

The Sun in conjunction with—

VENUS
: Strong love of pleasure, albeit a courteous, affectionate disposition, yet one that is easily influenced.

EXOTERIC ASTROLOGY

MERCURY Intuitive, ambitious mind that can be relied upon.
MOON Aspiring inner consciousness, if otherwise well aspected. The Ego can control the personality if both Luminaries are placed in a subjective house or above the horizon.

OPPOSITIONS OR SQUARE ASPECTS

NEPTUNE

Neptune afflicting—

URANUS Erratic moods resulting in sudden, perverse actions.
SATURN Cold nature inclined to suffer through misunderstandings, or revenge at the hands of others.
JUPITER Loss of friends leading on to mystical interests and profound realizations regarding fundamentals.
MARS Changeable, unreliable disposition; apt to become quarrelsome and discontented.
SUN Liability to losses through fraud financially, and through psychic conditions if interested in such matters.
VENUS Unsympathetic nature, strange feelings in emotional affairs : possessing little vitality.

THE ASPECTS

MERCURY Subtle mind tending to practise deliberate deception.
MOON Moody, psychic tendencies, inclined to become morbid.

URANUS

Uranus afflicting—

SATURN Reversals of a sudden nature alternating with numerous frustrations. The will is often weak also.
JUPITER Strange feelings aroused through unusual situations or ideas.
MARS Erratic, restless, eccentric disposition, inclined to extremes, both emotionally and physically.
SUN Fluctuating fortune, combined with separations and disasters. Emotional affairs turn out badly as a rule.
VENUS Easily influenced by others and liable to erratic disastrous love affairs of an unusual nature.
MERCURY Liability to sudden errors in judgment. The mind is difficult to convince when wrong.
MOON Sudden losses will come through strangers causing erratic decisions and Bohemian tendencies. The mind is unsettled and wilful.

EXOTERIC ASTROLOGY

SATURN

Saturn afflicting—

JUPITER Liability to heavy losses through ill-luck or lack of decision.
MARS The disposition is vindictive, uncompromising and foolhardy. Danger is threatened through accidents and trouble through financial associations.
SUN Selfish, solitary tendencies mar contacts with others. Losses are threatened through land or inheritance.
VENUS A jealous nature inclined to depression. Losses are possible through parents, marriage and financial affairs.
MERCURY The mind is suspicious, over-anxious and discontented. Losses may occur through theft, lack of initiative or fear.
MOON The disposition is peevish and apprehensive. Losses occur through want of enterprise or ill-health.

JUPITER

Jupiter afflicting—

MARS Wasteful, cynical tendencies mar the life, which will be subject to impulsive actions and folly.
SUN The disposition is pleasure-loving and

THE ASPECTS

prodigal. Friends will cause losses, leading to legal trouble.
VENUS   Luxurious nature inclined to extravagance. The mind is insincere, given to flattery and doubtful taste.
MERCURY A wavering nature, lacking in discrimination, subject to losses through legal matters or letters.
MOON   An over-confident, thriftless disposition liable to losses through the opposite sex and gambling.

MARS

Mars afflicting—

SUN   Headstrong, self-willed disposition, subject to losses through recklessness, speculation, accidents and the opposite sex.
VENUS   Sensuous, fickle, impulsive tendencies result in losses through the opposite sex and reckless living.
MERCURY An active, daring nature impatient of others' ideas, sometimes suffers losses through impulse, litigation or reckless projects.
MOON   Headstrong, contentious mind creates difficulties through hasty actions or tactlessness.

EXOTERIC ASTROLOGY

THE SUN

Sun afflicting—

MOON　　The mind alternates between hasty and irresolute conduct. Thus troubles arise through bad judgment or indecision. The health will be uncertain.

　　　　The Sun cannot form afflictions with Venus or Mercury. Nor can these two planets seriously afflict each other.

VENUS

Venus afflicting—

MOON　　Sensuous, improvident, erratic ways lead to folly through dissipation or indolence.

Mercury afflicting—

MOON　　A changeful, impractical mind makes errors through correspondence and unbusinesslike ways.

BENEFIC ASPECTS: TRINES AND SEXTILES

NEPTUNE

Neptune in benefic aspect to—

URANUS　Considerable ability for occult studies. Thus the life will be an unusual one.

THE ASPECTS

SATURN A cold nature possessing remarkable powers of concentration upon things that interest the mind, but not otherwise.

JUPITER An hospitable disposition, apt to be extravagant through over-generosity.

MARS. Remarkable personal magnetism. The mind is inclined to be sensuous and go to extremes.

VENUS A powerful emotional temperament possessing great devotion, if otherwise well aspected.

SUN A mystical mind, capable of grasping fundamental truths.

MERCURY Literary and inspirational powers which should lead to fame if otherwise well supported.

MOON The disposition is fanciful and impressionable but a little too negative.

URANUS

Uranus in benefic aspect to—

SATURN Gives intuition and a mystical or occult mind, capable of concentration and planning ahead.

JUPITER A fearless, resourceful nature. Unusual love affairs. Success through Uranian occupations.

EXOTERIC ASTROLOGY

MARS
: The mind is quick, original and enterprising. Gain is likely through inventions and journeys.

SUN
: A powerful mind possessing considerable magnetism, preserving the health in old age also. Gain through public appointments.

VENUS
: An original, intuitive mind, interested in occult subjects. Good fortune through friends and the public.

MERCURY
: An alert, scientific mind. Promising benefit through study or unusual mental pursuits.

MOON
: An original mind. Unusual occupations and methods of healing bring unexpected benefits.

SATURN

Saturn in benefic aspect to—

JUPITER
: A profound, philosophical mind possessing considerable concentration. Success through business judgment.

MARS
: A fearless, self-reliant and discriminating nature. Capable of concentrating upon a definite goal.

SUN
: A persistent, subtle yet sincere mind. Gain through property and financial ability.

THE ASPECTS

VENUS
: Sincere, aloof, persevering nature, capable of enduring sustained frustration (if otherwise afflicted).

MERCURY
: Adroit, persistent and impartial mind. Some possibilities of distinction in scientific or secretarial work.

MOON
: Reserved, careful and patient disposition. Inclined to be apprehensive at times.

JUPITER

Jupiter in benefic aspect to—

MARS
: Generous nature, a confident mind desiring to command. Gain through legacies and relatives.

SUN
: Hopeful, genial nature. The mind is philanthropic and discriminative. Gain is likely through investments, public appointments, etc.

VENUS
: Sociable, benevolent disposition. Success is likely through general popularity and good judgment.

MERCURY
: Cordial and discriminating mind, particularly intuitive regarding religious thought. Gain is possible through literary or business ability.

MOON
: A sincere and fortunate disposition. Success is promised through fortunate undertakings.

EXOTERIC ASTROLOGY

MARS

Mars in benefic aspect to—

SUN — Vital, enterprising, determined personality. Gain is likely through military or surgical skill, also through positions of authority.

VENUS — Susceptible, adventurous, demonstrative and sensuous disposition. Success is possible through the opposite sex or through artistic expression.

MERCURY — Ingenious, expeditious, shrewd and enthusiastic mind. Success is attained through speech, mental enterprise and swiftness of action.

MOON — Changeable, yet energetic nature. Success is probable through " cheek " and enterprise.

THE SUN

Sun in benefic aspect to—

MOON — Healthy and fortunate temperament. The mind is persevering and capable. Gain is likely through fortunate investments, government posts or social influence. There will be considerable ambition.

Neither Venus nor Mercury can form trines or sextiles to the Sun.

THE ASPECTS

VENUS

Venus in benefic aspect to and conjunction with—

MERCURY An affable, humorous and diplomatic mind. Gain is promised through art, music, the drama or literary gifts, especially in connexion with young people.

MOON Receptive, accomplished and artistic mind. The disposition is agreeable, attractive and affectionate. Women will prove helpful, and a certain amount of success is possible with the public.

MERCURY

Mercury in benefic aspect to and conjunction with—

MOON Subtle, adroit and imitative mind, capable of correct intuitions. Gain is probable through journalistic ability and the general public.

CHAPTER VI

THE LUMINARIES IN RELATION TO THE SIGNS

IT is an astrological tradition that the twelve houses govern fate and environment. Similarly it is also believed that the twelve signs are co-related to the twelve houses and these become the overtone and colour the twelve divisions of the chart with an individual excellence or limitation characteristic of each sign. Therefore the signs are related more to the inner disposition than outer circumstances.

The four elements, as expressed through the twelve signs, are strengthened by the Sun and rendered more positive, especially if the Sun be in fixed signs or the element fire. The Moon tends to have the opposite effect and weakens the sign, unless it is placed in Cancer or the sign of its exaltation Taurus. There are numerous combinations and permutations that can be created by combining Sun and Moon in various signs, thereby forming aspects or not as the case may be. Alan Leo has considered in detail these possibilities in *A Key to Your Own Nativity*.[1]

Other astrologers, including Sepharial, ignore

[1] In 1919 a well-known astrologer told me he considered Leo's Solar-Lunar variations in this book his finest achieve-

LUMINARIES IN RELATION TO THE SIGNS

these occurrences. In a book of this nature, which endeavours to stress the Zodiacal types as seen through the ascendant, the Luminaries will only be taken in relation to the various houses and not with regard to the signs.

When forming strong aspects to the cusp of the ascendant, however, they should be noted, for then they will combine in influencing the appearance according to the characteristics of the sign they are in and the rising sign, especially if operating from the mid-heaven.

THE SIGNS CONSIDERED AS ELEMENTS

As has been stated before, the fiery signs correspond to the spirit of man, the airy to his mind, the watery to his emotions, the earthy to his physical body. When the majority of planets are in fiery signs, the *spirit* or will has considerable influence over the chart, according to aspects and house position. Should the majority be in airy signs, then the mind has the greatest influence, if in the watery signs, then the emotions sway the actions, and if the earthy signs contain the majority, then the *physical body* is where the con-

ment. In 1935 I gave the book to a young couple, but they were unimpressed and said "the psychology was old-fashioned". Modern types respond more to the influence of Uranus and Neptune. Alan Leo foresaw this metamorphosis, for in his later writings the Sun and Moon are considered as "masks" for the more individual Uranus and Neptune respectively.

sciousness is chiefly focused. The grouping of the signs and elements in the foregoing manner enables the reader of the chart to develop a Zodiacal sense.

THE FIERY SIGNS

Aries is an impulsive and sometimes disruptive sign, combining force, energy and enthusiasm. The disposition is militant, enterprising, independent and assertive. It is best expressed through pioneering, whether mental or physical. The unevolved Aries man endeavours to carry out too many new ideas or schemes at one time. He is also inclined to embark upon fresh enterprises without considering their ultimate possibilities.

Leo people endeavour to centralize the will, and in advanced types to preserve the energies also. Thus many organizers or rulers are born under this sign. The disposition is generous and warm-hearted. The less evolved Leos are often dissipated but rarely utterly dissolute. The inner fire ultimately asserts itself through the fixed quality of the sign, and so the spirit dominates matter.

Sagittarius, being a mutable sign, gives the power in the advanced type to pass from one state of consciousness to another; from physical activity to mental inspiration or correct flashes of intuition. Hence this is the sign of the prophet. The lower type is chiefly interested in sport or " speeding " and is usually very restless physically.

LUMINARIES IN RELATION TO THE SIGNS

AIRY SIGNS

Libra, being an airy sign, is connected with the mind. In the advanced type there is the power to separate the mind from the senses, and balance one against the other. With these people neither the higher nor the lower mind predominates, and so there is always a tendency to "sit on the fence". In the unadvanced, poise or balance is lacking in the nature, and so partnership with others—possessing these qualities—becomes an ever-present essential.

Aquarius represents concentration of mind in the advanced type; a power to attain fixed mental stability and detached realization of abstract truth possessed by the Indian Yogi or a Western philosopher. The unadvanced go to the opposite extreme, and are usually at the mercy of their nervous moods of unrest which threaten to cause an emotional upheaval at any moment. Such people are extremely egotistical as opposed to the selfless search for truth inspiring the advanced *Aquarian*.

Gemini is dualistic and is able to transfer the mind from the concrete to the abstract in the advanced type. The lesser evolved become immersed in immediate interests of the moment, dropping one for another in an eager search for interesting facts or stimulating situations of an amusing kind.

EXOTERIC ASTROLOGY

WATERY SIGNS

Cancer is the first of the psychic trinity and has the power to reflect truth as in a mirror, in the controlled type. These make marvellous mediums. The unadvanced type possesses a keen desire for personal sensations of all kinds. Polarized mentally, there is the power to reflect the past, and thus able Cancerians make meticulous historians. The unadvanced merely shirk the difficulty of living under modern conditions. These people retire into their shell or secluded home as much as possible, feeling strangely defenceless everywhere else.

Scorpio has the power to control the emotions through the will, which can become a powerful internal occult force in the advanced type. The unevolved merely give way to desire in a somewhat reckless fashion, frequently dragging others down in the process. Both types are exceedingly intense and so are capable of going to extremes either way.

Pisces, being the last sign of the Zodiac, can become the " Universal Solvent " through a sense of sympathetic psychic union with others. In its highest sense this power of universal spiritual understanding was expressed in the life of the Christ and his saints. In the unadvanced types the negative and mediumistic tendencies of this

LUMINARIES IN RELATION TO THE SIGNS

sign lead to drifting or drunkenness. These people possess but little practical ability or even interest in mundane matters.

EARTHY SIGNS

Capricorn is associated with earthy aims or desires, accompanied with considerable ability along practical lines. In the advanced type these tendencies may run to extremes, this being a cardinal or active sign. These people worship established conventions or temporal power to the exclusion of almost everything else, and so become toadies or time-servers. The advanced type seeks to serve humanity along practical lines of reform and are capable of giving a lifetime to such work. Many successful politicians are also born under this sign.

Taurus gives strength and solidity, especially in connexion with practical affairs. People born under this sign possess considerable intuition for financial matters as well as the ability to retain wealth when gained or inherited. Taurians achieve success through concentration upon the fruits of this world. In the unevolved type this capacity tends to dominate everything else. The advanced type, however, seeks to aid others through financial help both individually and through public bodies.

Virgo is chiefly expressed through criticism and

EXOTERIC ASTROLOGY

discrimination as applied to mundane matters. The unevolved are censorious to subordinates and subservient to those holding authority. The higher type seeks knowledge through impersonal analysis.

VARIOUS DISEASES TO WHICH EACH RISING SIGN IS SUBJECT

♈ The head and face are the most liable to suffer. Especially through accidents, cuts, scars, toothache, neuralgia and vertigo if Aries is afflicted.

♉ The throat is the chief difficulty leading to diphtheria, quinsy or fits, if seriously afflicted.

♊ The lungs and chest are the chief trouble, resulting in consumption, bronchitis, brain fever and nervous disorders.

♋ The digestion and stomach are easily affected, leading to gastric ulcers, dropsy or even cancer.

♌ The heart, back and loins cause trouble, resulting in spasms, palpitations, fevers, etc. If much afflicted, jaundice, rheumatic fever and heart disease are possible.

♍ The bowels are weak and lead to colic, dysentery in some cases and chronic constipation in others. In extreme cases tuberculosis of the bowels is threatened.

♎ The kidneys and bladder are easily deranged. In extreme cases diabetes and Bright's disease are likely.

LUMINARIES IN RELATION TO THE SIGNS

♏ Piles, gravel, rupture and venereal diseases accompany this sign when afflicted. Also fistulas, blood-poisoning and unusual diseases if Mars is adversely aspected.

♐ Fevers, tumours and rheumatism are possible. When extremely afflicted, tuberculosis, violent accidents and injury to the thighs are likely.

♑ Rheumatism, eczema, and in extreme cases arthritis.

♒ The illnesses are chiefly nervous and frequently incurable.

♓ Sickness through damp feet, impure blood and inadequate ductless glands from birth are likely. This sign is never strong.

RISING PLANETS IN CONNEXION WITH THE CAREER AND THE HEALTH

Rising planets when in the *first* house have a powerful influence both on the appearance and the career; if within the first house they may be even more powerful than the Luminaries if the latter be weakly placed by sign or house. Taken in order as follows :

Neptune rising gives psychic ability when well aspected and undesirable mediumistic tendencies when afflicted. The fortunes are usually uncertain and largely depend upon the personal magnetism of the individual with this position at birth.

EXOTERIC ASTROLOGY

The disposition is usually artistic but negative and unstable, yet sensitive and open to the prevailing ideas of the time. Advanced types are mystical and extremely sympathetic. When afflicted there is danger of obsession.

Uranus rising is a positive influence, the mind reaches out eagerly towards new thought or pioneering work. There is usually a keen love of astrology, metaphysics or scientific study of a modern type. No matter what the Uranian takes up his mind will be in advance of the average. Thus he becomes subject to sudden upheavals and estrangements, and the career is liable to unexpected changes, sometimes necessitating an entirely new occupation. Regarding health, the system is liable to nervous disorders which can only be cured through electricity or massage.

Saturn rising is usually unfortunate unless well aspected. The life is restricted and the temperament melancholy and subject to numerous disappointments. It promises success through land or property, also through work that is laborious. Sickness arises through poor circulation, rheumatism or insufficient nourishment, for people under this influence are frequently indifferent to food.

Jupiter rising rules the law, the church, banks, colleges and other established positions. It gives power and dignity both to the body and the career, being the planet of " greater fortune ".

LUMINARIES IN RELATION TO THE SIGNS

Regarding health, difficulties sometimes arise through plethora or the spleen and liver get out of order.

Mars rising inspires soldiers, surgeons and active workers of all kinds. The disposition is confident and frequently essays several occupations at one time or in succession to each other. When rising it reacts upon the muscular system, rendering the body open to feverish complaints. When afflicted, accidents are likely.

Venus rising influences artists, musicians, actors, first-class stores of all kinds, large hotels and restaurants. The emotional affairs of both sexes are likely to influence the career considerably, which may become seriously handicapped if this planet is afflicted. When rising and afflicted the generative system in women is apt to suffer. In men the sympathetic system causes complications which react upon the health and are difficult to eradicate.

The Sun rising usually gives the support of influential people and a career is sought where such help is more easily obtained. Government positions are likely or the stage may prove successful. The disposition is generous, self-confident and sanguine. The Sun usually gives great vitality, but when afflicted there is likely to be heart trouble, especially after middle life.

Mercury rising inspires writers, thinkers and

those concerned with commercial enterprises requiring initiative. Orators also come under this planet, when operating from the ascendant. The mind is quick, subtle, talkative and restless, and so when rising reacts upon the body. Nervous troubles are likely and the mind will be subject to mental disorders. If this planet is afflicted the career is subject to set-backs.

The Moon influences sailors, travellers, those desirous of change, mystery or strange situations. In a more prosaic sense the Moon is concerned with the general public, such as nurses, male and female officials, service of varying kinds, etc. When well aspected there may be some public recognition, but this rarely endures and is liable to periods of unpopularity. With regard to health, it causes dropsical complaints; if seriously afflicted, gland trouble and indigestion.

THE DECANATES

The twelve signs of the Zodiac are divided into three equal parts, of ten degrees each, making thirty-six decanates. Each of these is ruled over by a planet. Put briefly, the second and third decanates take on the qualities of the successive signs of the particular *element* concerned. Thus the second decanate of Aries takes on the qualities of Leo, the next fiery sign. The third decanate would combine the qualities of Aries and Sagit-

LUMINARIES IN RELATION TO THE SIGNS

tarius, and so on throughout the Zodiac. These qualities are considered with relation to the illustrations depicting the various types according to their decanate influence.

CHAPTER VII

THE TWELVE RISING SIGNS AND DECANATE INFLUENCES

ALTHOUGH there are other influences such as the Sun, Moon and ruler of the ascendant which also affect the rising sign, the close study as an artist of the various Zodiacal types for over twenty-five years has led me to the conclusion that the decanate influences are the more powerful. To amplify these further by including other combinations of types would be to complicate matters by over-elaboration of the main theme. The eye is not capable of taking in more than a certain amount at one time, even if trained to observe things closely.[1]

The Sun, Moon and ruler of the ascendant undoubtedly affect the appearance if in the midheaven or throwing aspects to the rising degree.

[1] According to a film critic, the public is not capable of memorizing more than a limited number of film stars at one time. If new stars suddenly attract general attention, some of the older ones inevitably disappear into obscurity. The artistic life of a film star is rarely more than three to five years in consequence.

THE TWELVE RISING SIGNS

Similarly rising planets modify the appearance of the rising sign. For instance, the Sun and Jupiter increase both its vitality and girth ; whilst Saturn and Uranus have the opposite effect, the former inclined to increase the bony structure and the latter the nervous force ; Mars adds energy and muscular power ; the Moon, Venus and Neptune tend to have the reverse effect, giving a negative or lymphatic tendency to the body and the temperament.

Marked types, such as those depicted by fixed signs rising, for instance, are rarely much modified by either the Luminaries, rising planets or the position of the ruler, especially if any of these influences are in mutable or negative signs.

THE RISING SIGN

THE THREE DECANATES

ARIES

The first decanate of Aries, ruled by Mars, confers a frank disposition combined with a somewhat aggressive spirit. People born under this sign make fine pioneers and reformers, are always independent and sometimes clever. Being both active in quality and fiery in element, the Aries type is never happy unless " functioning collectively " for some ideal or urging others to do likewise. This quality seems to be increased rather than weakened through a lack of humour which is so characteristic of this sign, for it reinforces the belief in an individual destiny.

APPEARANCE OF THE FIRST DECANATE

The Aries type is usually of medium height, rather thin, with a long neck and sloping shoulders. The head is long, the forehead high and wide, the hair thick, dark and wiry. The eyebrows are bushy and the eyes deep-set ; the cheek-bones high and the nose aquiline. There are often strong lines from the nose to the corner of the mouth in middle age. The mouth itself is usually wide, set above a narrow, yet firm chin.[1] The body is long, strong and very straight in the back with a jutting-out pelvis. This spinal development seems to be a concomitant of untiring energy, and therefore Aries men often make the best long-distance runners.

THE SECOND DECANATE OF ARIES

The *Leo* decan is ruled by the Sun, and gives greater scope for the emotions. The disposition is prouder than that of the first decan and there is usually a strong love of display. Favours from men are likely, for this type always " plays the game " according to recognized standards. The ambitions become expressed through government

[1] See Aries in frontispiece.

posts. Success is likely along these lines, for the mind is fair in all dealings with others, and despises mean and underhand actions.

No. 1

APPEARANCE OF THE SECOND DECANATE

This is a more elegant figure than that of the first decanate. A similar head formation and narrow shoulders, but the body is less rigid and suggests the elegant waist-line usually associated with Leo as a rising sign.

THE THIRD DECANATE OF ARIES

The *Sagittarius* decanate of Aries is ruled by Jupiter. This gives strong passions, accompanied by a love of pleasure. This is not a fortunate decan, for it makes the disposition too impulsive and hasty at critical moments of the life. There are usually many friends and associates who considerably influence the outlook on life.

No. 2

APPEARANCE OF THE THIRD DECANATE

The face and eyes resemble the Sagittarius type, with the upward tilt to the eyelids, but the figure and head formation are those of Aries.[1]

[1] See illustration.

No. 1.
Leo decanate of Aries.

No. 2.
Sagittarius decanate of Aries.

THE TWELVE RISING SIGNS

TAURUS

The first decanate of Taurus is ruled by Venus. It gives a love of beauty and the arts. The disposition is slow to change, and somewhat indolent, yet people born under this sign usually acquire money either through their own efforts or those of others. Afflicted Taurians rarely trust men or circumstances, and so appear to dread the possible loss of their possessions more than other signs. The mind is practical, stolid and persistent, evincing strong likes and dislikes for both people and things. There is a persistent desire for comfort and personal success.

APPEARANCE OF THE FIRST DECANATE

People born under this sign are usually short, squarely built, yet with slender limbs and tapering fingers. The face is usually wide, the eyes full and somewhat cow-like. The lips and nostrils are also wide, although sensitive. The girl depicted here is typical of the shorter Taurian type.[1]

THE SECOND DECANATE OF TAURUS

The *Virgo* decanate of Taurus is ruled by Mercury. It gives appreciation of music, and usually acquires money and social position through the efforts of others. This is achieved subconsciously

---
[1] See Taurus in frontispiece.

through benefic aspects. The mind is matter-of-fact and sometimes detached, possessing considerable discrimination, intuition and artistic ability.

No. 3

APPEARANCE OF THE SECOND DECANATE

Note the wide Taurus face, but the tall figure of Virgo, also the slightly prominent " Hapsburg " underlip which almost invariably accompanies a strong Virgo influence upon the ascendant. The walk has a certain self-conscious elegance so frequent with a strong Virgo influence.

THE THIRD DECANATE OF TAURUS

The *Capricorn* decanate of Taurus, ruled by Saturn, makes the mind over-cautious and less intuitive than the others. The strong desire to be loved is frustrated through the earthy inability to sense correctly the outlook of either sex. It tends to ruin love affairs and home conditions generally in consequence. The life is under a cloud, despite strong powers of feeling and fidelity. There is but little power to break away from early training or the parents' psychology.

No. 4.　　　　　　　　No. 3.
Capricorn decanate of Taurus.　　Virgo decanate of Taurus.

EXOTERIC ASTROLOGY

No. 4

APPEARANCE OF THE THIRD DECANATE

Note the wide Taurus shoulders yet leaden expression, associated sometimes with a strong Saturn influence and often with Capricorn rising. The body is rarely tall with this decanate.

GEMINI

The first decanate is ruled by Mercury. This combination gives a kind and willing nature, an intellectual mind influenced by advanced thought. Yet there is often a certain wrong-headedness, which stands in the way of material success. The disposition is clever, versatile, nervous although stimulating. Men born under this sign make excellent journalists and love to influence others into their way of thinking.

APPEARANCE OF THE FIRST DECANATE

Geminians are usually tall and slight, with long arms, hands and fingers. The face is thin and sometimes hatchet-shaped, both the nose, which is often aquiline, and the chin being prominent. The mouth is well shaped with a pressed-out appearance of the lips. The eyes are wide-set, the complexion good. The brow is broad and the hair plentiful. The body is short in comparison with the legs, carried somewhat rigidly, particularly as to the shoulders, which are very flat and often high and wide. The women of this type often have rather masculine voices although feminine and smart in appearance.[1]

THE SECOND DECANATE OF GEMINI

The *Libra* decanate of Gemini is ruled by Venus. This combination gives artistic ability, quick perception, but lacks continuity. The talents are thus often misapplied, either through a general unsettled feeling or else through lack of self-esteem.

No. 5

APPEARANCE OF THE SECOND DECANATE

The lack of self-esteem is phrenologically revealed in the drawing of this decanate by the falling away at the back of the head. The figure is characteristic of the sign Libra rather than Gemini, being short-necked, and is likely to become stout in middle life.

THE THIRD DECANATE OF GEMINI

The *Aquarius* decanate of Gemini is ruled by Saturn. This influence gives greater success than the previous decanates, if Saturn be well aspected at birth, thereby obtaining help through old people. This combination gives greater depths to the sign

[1] See Gemini in frontispiece.

and the subconscious reacts upon the conscious mind through intuitive flashes. Success is sometimes attained through the expression of the emotions in a restrained way.

No. 6
APPEARANCE OF THE THIRD DECANATE

The example here shown combines the height of the Gemini decanate with that of the Aquarian man at his best, and often resembles the Gemini decanate of Aquarius.

CANCER

The first decanate is ruled by the Moon. This gives a dreamy, receptive, yet tenacious disposition, much influenced by family ties and limitations. The character is changeable, reserved, sensitive and imbued with considerable tenacity of purpose. People born under this sign make excellent biographers, being able to look up past history and re-live the lives of famous people they are portraying. In order to do this efficiently, they retire into the fastnesses of their homes and shut out, as much as possible, contemporary thought and activity. Great lovers of romance, the modern world appears to them both crude and ruthless; thus they live either in the past or through their own dreams in order to escape mundane facts.

No. 5.
Libra decanate of Gemini.

No. 6.
Aquarius decanate of Gemini.

EXOTERIC ASTROLOGY

The late Sir J. M. Barrie was a typical Cancerian, both in appearance and character.[1]

THE SECOND DECANATE OF CANCER

The *Scorpio* decanate of Cancer is ruled by Mars. The Mars influence gives greater will-power, acquisitiveness and desire for conventional success. There is also much curiosity regarding the lives of others, which sometimes leads to gossip and errors of judgment through too free-speaking.

No. 7

APPEARANCE OF THE SECOND DECANATE

Here the Mars influence affects the appearance as well as the disposition. The brain, however, is not equal to the demands made upon it by the enormous self-esteem revealed at the top of the head. The eyes are too close-set and the expression wary and frequently furtive. The nose is also Scorpionic rather than Cancerian.

THE THIRD DECANATE OF CANCER

The *Pisces* decanate of Cancer is ruled by Jupiter. In advanced types a strong love of travelling and adventure soon lead to an interest in occult or psychic pursuits. These people experience many changes and upheavals in their

[1] See frontispiece for feminine type of Cancer.

No. 7.
Scorpio decanate of Cancer.

No. 8.
Pisces decanate of Cancer.

life, and thus often attain recognition as writers or travellers. Madame H. P. Blavatsky was born under this decanate.

No. 8

APPEARANCE OF THE THIRD DECANATE

This example resembles the sign Pisces rather than the pure Cancerian. Here the afflicted ruler has made existing conditions all but impossible. Thus drink has become an "escape-mechanism" from an otherwise hard life.

LEO

The first decanate of Leo is ruled by the Sun. These people, being both fixed and positive, are usually sure of themselves under all circumstances. The disposition is frank, proud and generous, but lordly in manner and fond of show and ostentation. The first decanate is less fortunate than the others and the life is handicapped by false pride, poverty and family difficulties. Thus the mind resents the restrictions caused by the surrounding conditions and so becomes austere and somewhat distrustful of others, yet apt to become assertive at the wrong time. If Saturn is afflicted the health will suffer through some hidden frustration or inhibition, for Saturn rules the opposite decanate of the sign Aquarius.

THE TWELVE RISING SIGNS

APPEARANCE OF THE FIRST DECANATE

The body is usually powerfully built, with large bones, yet shapely withal and of a good presence. The face is square, the eyes fine, although sometimes set rather close together. The mouth is well shaped, but often somewhat thin and severe in expression. The chest is full and the back has a considerable slope to it. The walk is upright and supple, suggesting the lion, monarch of all he surveys.[1]

THE SECOND DECANATE OF LEO

The *Sagittarius* decanate of Leo is ruled by Jupiter. This gives a kind and genial nature, with warm sympathies but a tendency to go to extremes. It thus weakens the will-power of the sign as a whole, especially if Jupiter is afflicted. In the case of a married man any success attained would depend largely upon the wife.

No. 9

APPEARANCE OF THE SECOND DECANATE

Note the small head, short body and long legs associated with Sagittarius rather than Leo. Yet this young man possesses the Leo nose, mouth and jaw formation. This decanate is almost invariably taller than the other two.

[1] See frontispiece.

EXOTERIC ASTROLOGY

THE THIRD DECANATE OF LEO

The *Aries* decanate of Leo is ruled by Mars. This combination gives a strong will and much drive, there being the latent ability to rule over others. The disposition is frank and open, fond of hazardous enterprises abroad. In the advanced types the head may enlighten the heart through flashes of intuition, which raise the emotions to a higher plane.

No. 10

APPEARANCE OF THE THIRD DECANATE

In the drawing here depicting this decanate we have an extreme Aries type. Note the formation of brow, nose, back and legs. There are fine types of both sexes born under this decan, although they are usually small and slight. King Charles I of England was born with the last degrees of Leo rising, containing Neptune close to the cusp of the ascendant; this weakened his will and increased the physical sensitiveness to surrounding conditions. It also gave him strong aesthetic tastes.

VIRGO

The first decanate is ruled by Mercury. This indicates a reserved, receptive and orderly mind with but little scope for mundane success. The

No. 9.
Sagittarius decanate of Leo.

No. 10.
Aries decanate of Leo.

81

EXOTERIC ASTROLOGY

disposition is apt to be self-centred, secretive and melancholy. Yet Virgos are often witty but rarely positive, and so do not dominate their environment or fellow-men. Charles II of England and ex-King Alfonso of Spain had Virgo rising and endeavoured to manipulate their political difficulties. Mozart and Chopin are good examples of the retiring type.

APPEARANCE OF THE FIRST DECANATE

Virgo gives a slight, sensitive, sometimes elegant body, which is often tall as in the case of Charles II. The eyes are fine, but melancholy, the nose sometimes aquiline, and the mouth with a full under-lip. Like other mutable signs (Gemini, Sagittarius and Pisces), the body is short in comparison with the legs, and often slightly stoops when walking. The hair is plentiful and usually dark.[1]

THE SECOND DECANATE OF VIRGO

The *Capricorn* decanate of Virgo is ruled by Saturn. This combination usually gives an artistic mind possessing musical and literary tastes. The nature is genial yet retiring and somewhat reserved. The family fortunes tend to suffer at the end of life, which comes more and more under the influence of Saturn. The mind is too self-

[1] See frontispiece for masculine Virgo type.

THE TWELVE RISING SIGNS

centred to make satisfactory contacts with others of either sex, largely through the earthy inability to intuit their minds or emotions correctly.

No. 11
APPEARANCE OF THE SECOND DECANATE

Note the Hapsburg under-lip and also the sloping shoulders of Capricorn rather than the square ones associated with the first decanate. The voice is also (in this case) influenced by the latter sign, being harsh and discordant. Usually the two other decanates of Virgo, like Taurus people, possess soft voices and good enunciation.

THE THIRD DECANATE OF VIRGO

The *Taurus* decanate of Virgo is ruled by Venus. This gives an alert mind, combining artistic capacity with business ability or shrewdness if Mercury be well aspected. When this planet is afflicted there is often a tendency to indulge in shifty ventures, or by picking the brains of others.

No. 12
APPEARANCE OF THE THIRD DECANATE

The physique is clearly Taurian, with a tendency to stoutness in middle life. The eyes also resemble that sign and there is no indication of a " Hapsburg " under-lip. On the whole this is the most fortunate of the three decanates.

LIBRA

The first decanate is ruled by Venus. This gives a refined but kindly nature, easily influenced by others. Thus the life will be subjected to numerous changes, initiated chiefly by the desires of others, whilst the mind halts between two courses.[1] There is some chance of inheriting property or possessing land at the close of life. The mind is fond of comparing, whilst the career is often literary or artistic, but there is not much power to act individually or make decisions apart from others.

APPEARANCE OF THE FIRST DECANATE

Libra people are usually slender in youth, but tend to stoutness in middle life. The features are regular and pleasing, this being a sign of beauty, especially in women. The head has a characteristic falling away at the back, denoting lack of self-esteem, for Libra people rarely push themselves and depend upon their partners for many things. The brow is good, both broad and high, the mouth sensitive and well shaped. The

[1] This tendency is increased for those who have up to fifteen Libra rising, as Cancer and the Moon then rule the midheaven, thereby subjecting them to the mood of the moment and its influence.

No. 11.
Capricorn decanate of Virgo.

No. 12.
Taurus decanate of Virgo.

EXOTERIC ASTROLOGY

shoulders in men, however, are often too narrow and the figure too wide at the hips.[1]

THE SECOND DECANATE OF LIBRA

The *Aquarius* decanate of Libra is ruled by Saturn, which gives considerable success, often followed by a fall through lack of balance. The inner nature is somewhat aloof, owing to the Saturn influence, early poverty and family frustrations. Nevertheless, the ambitions will not be realized without the support of others; usually an alliance of business or emotional partnerships in succession, rather than friendship with several people at one time.[2]

No. 13

APPEARANCE OF THE SECOND DECANATE

The drawing depicting this decanate gives the short Libra neck and high shoulders associated with this sign. The Aquarian aquiline nose gives initiative and combativeness. The narrow hips are also Aquarian, resembling the Libra decanate of Aquarius (No. 22). Men born under this decanate, however, have wide hips as a rule, as was the case of Napoleon (who also possessed the Aquarian aquiline type of nose). Hitler has the wide-hipped male Libra figure, but his nose is

[1] See frontispiece.
[2] Both Napoleon I and Adolph Hitler had this decanate rising at birth.

No. 13.
Aquarius decanate of Libra.

No. 14.
Gemini decanate of Libra.

more Taurian, his ruler, Venus, being placed in that sign.

THE THIRD DECANATE OF LIBRA

The *Gemini* decanate of Libra is ruled by Mercury. The disposition is amiable yet baffling, refined but wanting in positivity. There is usually too much dependence upon others, often due to the lack of self-esteem so frequently revealed in the Libra head formation. This cranial development craves inspiring reassurance from the opposite sex.

As Mr. H. G. Wells says in *The Anatomy of Frustration* :

> One of the functions of a lover is to tell us we are "all right". This assurance cannot be given by casually encountered lovers. It can be done with full effectiveness only by a chosen person who has chosen to specialize in this service. At times this imaginative necessity is the very core of love. When the lover shows that he or she sees coldly and plainly, then the love affair is finished.

No. 14

APPEARANCE OF THE THIRD DECANATE

Compare this head with the Libra ascendant (first decan). Note the short neck but Gemini face and figure of this man. He would not be likely to get stout in middle life, but rather tend to Geminian thinness and nervousness.

THE TWELVE RISING SIGNS

SCORPIO

The first decanate is ruled by Mars. The character is daring, strong-willed, energetic and forceful, capable of considerable endurance and sustained effort. This applies to advanced types. The unadvanced are deceitful and treacherous, having no control over their desires. The body thus suffers through excess. There is considerable ability for self-dramatization and many born under this sign love to create an air of mystery around themselves. The mind is both brusque and critical and disinclined to flatter others.

APPEARANCE OF THE FIRST DECANATE

Scorpio people can be both thick-set and short, or tall, lithe and attenuated. Like other fixed signs (Taurus, Leo and Aquarius), they are rather long in the body. The features of this decan are often aquiline, the brows are prominent and the eyes intense in their gaze, the mouth close-set, the chin full and determined. Joan Crawford, the film star, has all the grace of the finer Scorpio type, whilst Mussolini combines the facial characteristics of the first decanate with the thicker body formation of the Pisces decanate, being ten degrees Scorpio rising (a Solar number).[1]

[1] See frontispiece for feminine type.

EXOTERIC ASTROLOGY

THE SECOND DECANATE OF SCORPIO

Ruled by Jupiter. The disposition is proud and haughty, although capable of rulership and considerable endurance. When afflicted there is a distinct tendency to become tyrannical and cruel. If supported by favourable planetary influences, fame and world recognition are likely.[1]

THE THIRD DECANATE OF SCORPIO

The *Cancer* decanate of Scorpio is ruled by the Moon. If the nativity is a refined one, this gives a strong love of psychic phenomena or mysticism. In other cases the love of sensation causes secret enmity of women who create difficulties in the life. The jealous tendencies are very strong.

No. 15

APPEARANCE OF PISCES-CANCER CUSP OF SCORPIO

Here a combination of two decanates is expressed in one individual, the degree of the ascendant being nineteen degrees Scorpio. This degree, in the case of all the twelve signs, contains the latent power to express both the rising sign and the two decanate influences, thereby enriching the nature and making it more complex.

In this case the Scorpio pride of spirit contends with the Pisces-Cancer love of psychic phenomena.

This decanate can be seen in the nativity of Mussolini.

No. 15.
Pisces-Cancer cusp of Scorpio.

EXOTERIC ASTROLOGY

Note that the body possesses the narrow hips of Scorpio, whilst the face and nose are of a Pisces type, wide and short, not long and aquiline. Yet this youth possesses the Scorpio eagle eye and the well-shaped slender hands and feet. The head, however, indicates Pisces ideality rather than Scorpio shrewdness and combativeness.

SAGITTARIUS

The first decanate is ruled by Jupiter. It denotes an open-minded, sympathetic, kindly disposition, inclined to be touchy if taken advantage of. When well aspected there is considerable intuition and mental independence ; when afflicted the mental powers become chaotic, resulting in restlessness and dissatisfaction.

APPEARANCE OF THE FIRST DECANATE

The Sagittarian body is usually tall, slender, well made and somewhat stooping. The neck is set far forward on the chest like a horse, the prototype of the first fifteen degrees. The eyes are fine, often hazel, the nose short, the mouth rather large and genial, the chin firm. The body is short-waisted and wide at the hips, the legs long and well shaped, making the whole figure graceful, possessing the easy swaying movement of the racehorse. Joel McCrea, the film actor, in appearance is typical of this decanate.

THE TWELVE RISING SIGNS

The *Aries* decanate of Sagittarius is ruled by Mars. When afflicted this combination increases the headstrong tendencies and so the body suffers through mental and physical exhaustion. When well aspected the mind is capable of making rapid adaptations to changing conditions. Legacies are possible and also help through influential people.

No. 16

APPEARANCE OF THE SECOND DECANATE

The young man with the *right* side of his face portrayed is the Sagittarian decanate of this sign, depicting another variety of the type indicated in the frontispiece. The head is longer both from the forehead to the chin and also from the front to the back. The figure resembles that of the frontispiece and also that of the Sagittarian decanate of Leo.

No. 17

The *Aries* decanate of Sagittarius has a more combative face. Note the equally developed powers of reflection, perception, combativeness, firmness, determination and resolution revealed to the phrenologist in the forehead, nose, upper lip and chin respectively. The figure resembles the Aries-Leo combination, for the shoulders are rather narrow and sloping, although the body is taller, thereby making a minor Zodiacal contrast with the first decanate of this sign, which usually has wide shoulders.

THE THIRD DECANATE OF SAGITTARIUS

This is the *Leo* decanate of Sagittarius. The passions are strong but under control, the mind sober and capable of great concentration. This is the human or better half of the sign, promising success and wealth after a period of difficulty. The life is much influenced by close friendships and business associates.

No. 18
APPEARANCE OF THE THIRD DECANATE

The *Leo* decanate of Sagittarius is illustrated by a portrait of the late Empress Eugenie. Here the face takes on some of the characteristics of the next sign Capricorn, which is usually intercepted in the first house for those born under this decan and therefore considerably influences the appearance as well as the point of view. This remarkable woman possessed the aloofness and dignity characteristic of the sign Leo, and was especially marked at the close of her life, spent in exile in England. The early part of it was wrecked by her Leo arrogance and lack of intuition ; a combination which helped to shatter her husband's precarious hold over the French

No. 16.	No. 18.	No. 17.
Sagittarius decanate of Sagittarius.	(Portrait.) Leo decanate of Sagittarius.	Aries decanate of Sagittarius.

nation. Her Sun, ruler of the sign Leo, was in Taurus in the fifth house, bringing the sudden publicity followed by scandal and unpopularity, so frequently concomitant with this position at birth.

Both Elizabeth Tudor and Benjamin Disraeli were born with this combination of Sagittarius and Capricorn. This gave them sudden fiery flashes from the superconscious mind combined with earthy guile, expressed through skilful manœuvring and subtle procrastination, masquerading as indecision. Both these remarkable people possessed the long face, drooping outer corners to the eyes and slight figure characteristic of the third decanate, in addition to the Leo ostentatious and somewhat daring way of dressing.

CAPRICORN

The first decanate is under Saturn and denotes an ambitious mind, possessing the power to rise above the early environment to positions of responsibility. Yet fears and doubts will hamper these achievements, for the nature is often lacking in sympathy and usually conventional in outlook. People of the older generation born under this sign seem frequently inclined to humourless merriment and goat-like caperings, alternating with fits of melancholy. Younger Capricornians

THE TWELVE RISING SIGNS

are far more free from inhibitions and complexes and so tackle their problems in a more straightforward fashion. There have been born under this sign fine types who were desirous of serving humanity, but their efforts were rarely free from personal aims. Gladstone possessed both the appearance and characteristics of this decan.

APPEARANCE OF THE FIRST DECANATE

The figure is usually thin and bony, possessing prominent features and a protruding chin. The neck is frequently short and thin, whilst the voice becomes harsh and unpleasing. The body is often short with narrow shoulders, which appear the more marked as the face is often far too large for the body. The eyes are small and lacklustre, the hands ugly. Elderly feminine members of this sign are frequently given to making spasmodic and even grotesque gestures in order to elaborate some commonplace incident, and they revel in the obvious, for nothing is too small for comment as far as they are concerned. Thus they appear as amazing phenomena of tedious restlessness to people born under other signs.[1]

THE SECOND DECANATE OF CAPRICORN

The *Taurus* decanate of Capricorn is ruled by Venus. This is a more fortunate combination

[1] See frontispiece.

than the previous one. Influential friends assist the career, which is dominated by a fixed desire to succeed, constrained by a more equable manner and kindly nature. When afflicted the nature takes on a fixed quality and the disposition becomes despotic.

No. 19

APPEARANCE OF THE SECOND DECANATE

This combination widens the figure and face and checks the restless expression of the sign, but the eyes often retain the blank lack-lustre appearance so frequently associated with Capricornians. In this case the voice is Taurian and therefore soft and pleasing. But the figure is more angular and rigid than the pure Taurian type.

THE THIRD DECANATE OF CAPRICORN

The *Virgo* decanate of Capricorn is ruled by Mercury. This influence quickens the mind though the disposition is usually melancholy and the early life is subject to numerous hardships and limitations. The conscious mind is chiefly concentrated upon facts and mundane details; the temperament resembles that of the local town clerk. For this type of mind rarely possesses much initiative or independence of thought.

No. 19.
Taurus decanate of Capricorn.

No. 20.
Virgo decanate of Capricorn.

No. 20

APPEARANCE OF THE THIRD DECANATE

Here the drooping eyelids and the raised eyebrows of the sign are well in evidence, also the sloping shoulders, the angular body and the Capricorn voice, which takes on a deeper Virgo tone through the decanate influence.

AQUARIUS

The first decanate is ruled by Saturn. In a strange way this takes on the quality of the opposite Solar sign, for the disposition is genial but somewhat easily led into sensational experiments. Probably due to the fact that many who have this decanate rising have the whole of Pisces intercepted in the first house. When well aspected there is usually considerable acumen and the life passes pleasantly. Yet the fate largely depends upon the associates. The character is humane and sometimes possesses the capacity to co-operate with others in philanthropic schemes, but only when remarkable ability is indicated elsewhere in the nativity.

APPEARANCE OF THE FIRST DECANATE

Some Aquarians are tall, slight and good-looking, with a well-shaped straight or aquiline nose and a rather receding chin.[1] When the

---

[1] See frontispiece for masculine type.

THE TWELVE RISING SIGNS

intercepted sign Pisces contains a planet, then the appearance takes on a Piscean look. The nose is short and the features irregular but pleasing, the figure shorter and often stout. The appearance as well as the character depends upon the position of Saturn.

THE SECOND DECANATE OF AQUARIUS

The *Gemini* decanate of Aquarius is ruled by Mercury. Here there is less tendency to drift. The mind becomes more active and interested in contemporary political or journalistic activities. When well aspected there is scientific ability and considerable depth of thought along mathematical or astrological lines. Ultimate recognition is likely, although the most advanced types will always be desirous of solitude.

No. 21

APPEARANCE OF THE SECOND DECANATE

Here we have the more extraverted type of mind born under this decanate, widely diffused in interest, desiring neither to monopolize nor to be monopolized. This man has the Aquarian's preference for celibacy and would not be likely to marry, unless to escape some emotional problem with which his mind would find it difficult to contend. Note the large perceptives as opposed to those of the next decanate, where the reflectives are the dominating influence of the brain.

THE THIRD DECANATE OF AQUARIUS

The *Libra* decanate of Aquarius is ruled by Venus. The disposition is melancholy and subject to moods and fancies. If afflicted, there may be strange visions or hallucinations. The mind is inclined towards mysticism and the fate is largely affected by marriage and love affairs, yet there is little satisfaction, as a rule, to be obtained through either. The Libra side demands love, yet the Saturnian element of the nature fears to trust fate, whilst at the same time the emotions are subjected to a form of self-analysis, which, in the end, destroys the thing it beloved. This decan, if afflicted, often causes nervous disorders.

No. 22

APPEARANCE OF THE THIRD DECANATE

Note the narrow hips and the upward tilt to the eyes and eyebrows. The subtle physical connexion between Scorpio and Aquarius is seen here, for both have the serpent for their symbol. Aquarius has two serpents, containing alternative extremes of development.[1] The square aspect

---

[1] The signs ♌ ♍ ♏ and ♒ all symbolize various conditions of the serpent and express various characteristics of that

No. 21.
Gemini decanate of Aquarius.

No. 22.
Libra decanate of Aquarius.

between these two signs is indicative of the mind endeavouring to comprehend and then control the emotions, a psychological conflict increasingly apparent with both sexes of a sensitive type now that the Libra decanate of Aquarius begins to affect the race-unconscious, as we move *backwards* from Pisces to Aquarius.[1]

influence. But the signs Scorpio and Aquarius take on, in some cases, the physical gliding movement and narrow supple body characteristic of the serpent.

[1] This phenomenon is due to the Precession of the Equinoxes. This precession was discovered by Hipparchus 120 B.C. on observing the difference in length of the year by two methods:

(1) from one equinox to the same equinox next year;

(2) by observing the position of the Sun with reference to the fixed stars and measuring the length of the year when the sun has again reached the same position. The length of the year measured by the first method is 20 m. 30 s. shorter than that measured by the second. The difference is due to a gradual shifting of the plane of the equator which causes the point of intersection of the equator with the ecliptic to move backwards so as to meet the Sun sooner in its eastern motion along the ecliptic. This retrograde motion of the equinoxial points, referred to as the precession of the equinoxis, is due to the fact that the pole of the equator swings slowly round the pole of the ecliptic, taking about 25,800 years to make one complete circle, moving at the rate of $50''\cdot2$ per annum. The first point of Aries thus moves backwards through the constellations of the Zodiac at the rate of $50''\cdot2$ per annum. More than 2,000 years ago the first point of Aries was actually in the constellation Aries, but now, owing to the precession of the equinoxes, it has moved through the constellation Pisces and is passing into Aquarius.

If the earth were a homogeneous sphere there would be no precession. The cause of precession is the attraction of the Sun and Moon on the equatorial portions of the earth, which bulge out above the true sphere, tending to pull the plane of

THE TWELVE RISING SIGNS

PISCES

The first decanate of Pisces is ruled by Jupiter. Dual experiences rule this sign. Like the other mutable signs, there is the possibility of two extremes of development. With the unevolved soul there is rarely much control over the emotions or the moods of the moment. The advanced soul, however, is capable of mystical realizations of a subtle order. The mind then becomes receptive to higher influences, instead of being dominated by anybody in the vicinity. If seriously afflicted, the nature is secretive, morbid and, in extreme cases, even corrupt.

Few Pisces people have much ambition and are only too often inclined to leave the world and its inhabitants to their own devices and find peace in a life of contemplation. The late Lord Rosebery was a Pisces type, possessing all its elusive and melancholy tendencies.

---

the equator into the plane of the ecliptic by attracting more powerfully those portions of the bulging part which are nearest to them. The effect of the tendency to draw the axis of the earth into perpendicularity with the plane of the ecliptic combined with the spinning round of this axis, is to make the end of the earth's axis turn in a circle round the axis of the ecliptic.

The first point of Aries is that point on the celestial equator where the Sun crosses it in Spring and is gradually moving ; for this reason the signs of the Zodiac do not correspond with the constellations of the Zodiac.

EXOTERIC ASTROLOGY

APPEARANCE OF THE FIRST DECANATE

Pisces people usually have large fishy eyes, set in a small sensitive pale face, and even when young, are bulky in body; doubtless the result of inadequate glands. Some are also clumsy in movement, turning their feet and flat insteps East and West as they shamble rather than walk. Yet so contrary is the sign that many born under it are light on their feet, in spite of their weight, and make excellent dancers.[1]

THE SECOND DECANATE OF PISCES

The *Cancer* decanate of Pisces is ruled by the Moon. This influence awakens the latent sensitiveness of the sign, giving internal aspirations, persistency and ability to use Pisces virtues and avoid its vices, provided the ascendant is reinforced elsewhere or through a particular degree rising. Such is the case with the youth (No. 23 illustration), who combines the best influence of both the second and third decanates.

THE THIRD DECANATE OF PISCES

The *Scorpio* decanate of Pisces is ruled by Mars. Here again the dual influence of the sign Pisces can be expressed in two ways. The unevolved are apt to be jealous, selfish and conventional,

[1] See frontispiece.

possessing a passionate desire for success at all costs. The life is therefore subject to serious reversals which are counteracted by the help of influential friends. Yet an inner urge for personal recognition and success will spur the nature along some reckless course with complete disregard of the consequences. This makes the mind hard, without much feeling. The advanced type would use the force of this decan and apply it to an inner mystical development, thereby achieving occult realizations of a high order.[1]

No. 23

APPEARANCE OF THE PISCES-CANCER-SCORPIO TYPE

Like the Pisces-Scorpio youth depicted elsewhere, this young man has nineteen degrees rising, thus combining three watery decanates. This is an equally subtle combination with mystical possibilities and the power to contact the forces of nature through solitary wanderings. Although this face is a Cancer type, the body possesses the long Scorpio back, narrow hips and shoulders, resembling the other muscular Martian sign Aries. Thus the wheel of physical manifestation comes back full circle in this Martian merging through decanate influence. The Mars body has a powerful

[1] Sagittarius, ruling the tenth house of Pisces people, gives considerable intuition along superconscious or subjective lines.

spinal development, as a rule, as well as a strong will. This combination of physical and psychic forces renders an advanced Mars man open to higher influences but capable of becoming immune to cruder objective stimuli.

Through subtle mystical realizations this young man, born within forty-eight hours of the January Lunation 1910, has experienced the cross aspects of the planets from cardinal signs and has risen above the necessity of Jung's complementary Persona shadow or Mr. Wells's " lover " to tell him he is " all right ". Reinforced by subtler unseen associations, he can dispense with " the confirmatory shadow " on this plane. Although young, he has already dimly sensed what Mr. H. G. Wells has taken a lifetime to realize and lately expressed through *The Anatomy of Frustration* that—

> There is really no weaving of the almost irresistible tendency to mix up the recurrent urgency of sex-desire with the ever-present need for that confirmatory " Yes ". That is why the personal love story will remain perennially unsatisfactory and perennially interesting. With our utmost efforts to imagine the contrary, personal relationships remain almost as accidental as food or the weather. They stimulate, they can surprise with an unexpected delightfulness, we cannot live without their happening, but they change and pass. We can no more arrest the happy moment than we can hold a lovely sunrise or sunset. The roving mind falls back at last upon a stoical self-identification with the specific man, upon self-forgetfulness in enduring work for the world community, as the one and only enduring refuge

No. 23.
Cancer-Scorpio cusp of Pisces.

from frustration. We have to make the best of that. Whether we accept it in a mood of religious exaltation or whether we accept it with a wry smile is our individual affair; that is how things are.

FROM PISCES TO AQUARIUS

The Zodiacal significance of the Changing Age is apprehended by the astrologer when he recollects that we are progressing backwards in an astrological sense from Pisces to Aquarius in a major cycle and from Mars to the Moon in a minor one.[1] Thus the merging of the Pisces Age into the Aquarian will be a marvellous opportunity to realize basic truths, contained within the race unconscious.

For the exceptional individual there is the way of the mystic, which can be created through the trine aspect Pisces forms with Scorpio, especially if he possesses the nineteen degrees decanate influence stressed elsewhere. For this Solar number enables the mind to free itself from present limitations (involved in the first decanate of every sign) and to project the mind forward or backward. Such psychological experience is described by Mr.

[1] This cycle is based upon counting thirty-five years to each day of the week and working backwards. On the 21st March, 1944, Mars day or Tuesday will be merged into a Moon day or Monday cycle lasting until 1979, when a Solar cycle is destined to close the twentieth century. If ♆ and ♅ are substituted for the ☽ and ☉, as Alan Leo did regarding the 35-year ♂ cycle, the earth will be under their strange and *sustained* influence from 1944–2014.

THE TWELVE RISING SIGNS

Dunne in his *Experiment with Time* and frequently induced by Indian and Western occultists with a view to studying a problem impersonally.[1]

This ability, associated with mutable signs, is essential if the higher consciousness is to be developed. For not until the will refuses to be diverted from its course by extraneous influences can the superconscious mind successfully contend with the conflicting inner desires or external stimuli influencing the conscious mind.

In *Adepts of the Five Elements*[2] the sub- or unconscious mind of Western psychologists is co-related to that centre called the " Web of Life " by Indian occult tradition and associated with the signs Libra-Virgo-Scorpio by me on page 34. On the next page the *modus operandi* of psycho-analysis is related to the sign Aquarius, while it is further suggested that the trine aspect between

[1] H. P. Blavatsky had 28° Cancer rising, the Solar number, and thereby became attuned to the universal etheric element latent in the Pisces decanate of Cancer and appertaining to the passing Age. Her mind became entirely absorbed in superconscious phenomena and she was able to project it backward or forward through a psychological identification with the superconscious Solar element in nature. In her next life, like everyone else, she will be subject to the peculiar limitations of the Libra decanate of the Aquarian Age; for the occult powers of the passing Age are rapidly becoming short-circuited. A close conjunction between the Sun and Neptune in Virgo might be used to achieve this subtle apotheosis in connection with the race-unconscious ($28 = 10$, $19 = 10$, $10 = 1$).

[2] Published in 1933.

Uranus and Neptune between 1938-41 will be used by advanced types to co-relate the subconscious with the conscious mind (through this unusual combination) in a physical way as earthy signs are involved. This trine aspect continues into Libra and Gemini from October, 1942, until June, 1945, which should prove beneficial for advanced types either born or working in the United States of America.

It cannot be over-stressed that as the Libra decanate of the sign Aquarius is the first of its airy decanates to react upon the earth as we move backwards from Pisces to Aquarius, the subconscious element in man is likely to be the *first* affected. Hence the necessity for developing control over that centre during the centuries to come.

A skilful analyst, working from *without*, may make a patient reveal the secrets of the subconscious, but only the patient's superconscious mind, operating from *within* and aware of his past as well as his future, can adequately cope with the aftermath of this revelation. Occultists of the future will doubtless evolve a way of freeing their pupils from inhibitions sufficiently for them to work for social service as advocated by Mr. Wells. Thus will the airy element in man become paramount and the *personal* element of the Libra influence be raised to the universal diffused interest latent in the sign Gemini.

DRAWN FROM LIFE

No. 24.

This boy possesses a tall Gemini figure combined with the Libra profile and head formation. He had 28° Libra rising, the Solar number, reinforced by the Sun and 26° of Scorpio within the first house. Through this combination there is the latent power to subordinate the personal element of Libra to the Geminian universally diffused interest in contemporary problems. This possibility is enhanced through Venus and Mercury in Sagittarius and the second house trine Neptune in Leo and the mid-heaven.

CHAPTER VIII

THE INFLUENCE OF THE PLANETS IN THE HOUSES

PLANETS IN THE FIRST HOUSE

NEPTUNE : Placed here gives psychic tendencies and clairvoyance in advanced types and undesirable mediumistic or receptive tendencies in the unevolved types. The latter form of negativity may lead to obsession if this planet is seriously afflicted.

Uranus : The disposition is erratic, obstinate and yet original. The mind is usually interested in occult or profound subjects. This planet causes sudden and unexpected estrangements, accidents, and complete changes either in the general outlook or in the profession.

Saturn : Gives industry and perseverance. The mind is cautious and apprehensive, the habits solitary. In advanced types there is considerable patience, but the unevolved are often harsh and melancholic.

Jupiter : Increases the girth and vitality, whilst mundane success is achieved along conventional

INFLUENCE OF THE PLANETS

lines. The advanced types are genial and kindly; the perverted Jupiterians are hypocritical or deliberate deceivers.

Mars : Gives strength and courage, considerable independence and recklessness. The unadvanced types are too domineering and self-assertive.

Venus : Denotes a disposition which is usually amiable and eager to please, fond of music and society. The advanced type studies art and higher thought, the lesser evolved become submerged in sensation in their search for true union.

Mercury : Gives an eager, curious mind; much travelling and enterprise. The advanced type are sometimes orators. Unevolved Mercurians are merely chatterers.

The Sun : Confers success, good health and a proud, somewhat ostentatious disposition. There is often a love of the drama, which may become expressed upon the stage in some way.

The Moon : Gives a strong desire for publicity without much power to sustain it professionally. There are often many reversals and changes when afflicted.

PLANETS IN THE SECOND HOUSE

Neptune : Denotes losses through speculation if afflicted, or money may be acquired in unusual or shady ways, such as doubtful company promoting. There may be successful gambling if well aspected.

EXOTERIC ASTROLOGY

Uranus: Foreshadows sudden financial losses if afflicted, and unexpected gains if well aspected. Money may be earned through astrology, unusual fiction, inventions, etc.

Saturn: A thrifty disposition which rarely benefits in the long run, unless well aspected. There may be gain through public appointments, contracts, antiques, or research work.

Jupiter: Promises gain through government posts, legal affairs or religious bodies. It gives success through influence particularly.

Mars: Money comes easily through enterprise and energies well expended, but is spent as freely. Farming, surgery, and the services come under this planet.

Venus: Indicates money earned through artistic pursuits: it is also spent freely by men upon women. For a woman there is financial gain through marriage if well aspected. Hotels, restaurants and high-class shops come under this planet.

Mercury: Denotes gain by literary appointments, speaking, travelling, commissions, dividends, etc. It is beneficial for commercial undertakings, such as advertising and publishing.

The Sun: Gives benefits through those possessing social influence, also through government appointments. The father is often wealthy and assists financially. But money is usually spent freely, especially if afflicted.

INFLUENCE OF THE PLANETS

The Moon: Indicates money is obtained through the mother or wealthy women if well aspected, also through the employment of labour. If afflicted, it indicates a subordinate position. The fortunes are subject to change, but there may be gain through holding some public post.

PLANETS IN THE THIRD HOUSE

Neptune: Denotes fanciful and strange mental realizations. Sometimes there is an interest in psychic matters. The mind is original and creative, but somewhat melancholic and unbalanced unless free from affliction. Psychic pursuits are best avoided.

Uranus: Gives an original mind, which is apt to operate somewhat erratically. Publications coming under this planet are unusual but often unpopular, being too advanced for the times. Trouble is frequent through correspondence and relatives become estranged.

Saturn: Indicates that difficulties arise through relatives, letters and publications. Travelling is apt to cause sickness and liable to disappointments. The mind is slow and suspicious if afflicted. Even when well aspected there is but little power to mentally contact others.

Jupiter: Gives a kindly but conventional mind, yet courteous and considerate of others in third-house matters. There is not much originality with this position at birth.[1]

Mars : In this case correspondence frequently causes friction, especially if Mars be afflicted. There may even be some litigation to contend with. Relatives may cause trouble and accidents are likely. The mind is quick but apt to lack poise.

Venus : The mind is artistic and kindly. If Venus be afflicted the mind is sensuous and too much inclined for superficial intercourse. Short journeys and correspondence are also favourable. Relations are helpful and fortunate.

Mercury : Is in a good position if in this house. The mind is alert, enterprising and often original. There should also be latent ability for journalism or original writings. Journeys should be many and successful.

The Sun : Indicates that creative work will frequently lead to success. The mind is austere, firm but magnanimous. Brothers or sisters may prove helpful. There may be some tendency to become patronizing if the Sun is afflicted.

The Moon : Denotes that the mind is changeable and lacking in continuity, yet curious regarding superficial matters. There are often short journeys or many changes of occupation or interests.

---

[1] Jupiter has the same colourless but vaguely benefic quality in the fifth house, but only if well aspected.

INFLUENCE OF THE PLANETS

PLANETS IN THE FOURTH HOUSE

Neptune: Indicates some unusual end to the life of a hampering nature. The early home conditions are rarely favourable and the body is always subject to psychic depletion, for often the houses visited prove physically exhausting, though this tendency is rarely realized at the time.

Uranus: Shows many changes and early unhappiness in the home life. There will be trouble through the parents and sudden reversals. In an advanced nativity mental illumination is likely at the close of life. If afflicted, a sudden end is possible.

Saturn: Indicates losses and frustration in all matters connected with this house. The early surroundings are rarely congenial. The life is hampered by fate, unless well aspected, when a refined form of asceticism at the close of life may illuminate the mind.

Jupiter: Is fortunate for gain by legacy and promises success at the close of life. Parents are helpful if this planet receives benefic aspects from either luminary. If this planet is afflicted there will be waste of money, or trouble through the parents and their affairs. If occultism is indicated elsewhere this position denotes an expansion of consciousness.

Mars: Causes trouble at the end of life, con-

EXOTERIC ASTROLOGY

flict in the home and many domestic disputes. If afflicted by Uranus, sudden troubles through property or accidents are likely. The end of life may be equally unexpected. The disposition is usually violent or uncontrolled, especially if Mars is afflicted.

Venus: Denotes an equable home, inheritance from parents and a happy end to life. All things tend to a successful issue, unless there are serious afflictions involving this planet, when extravagance or self-indulgence are likely.

Mercury: Indicates numerous changes and considerable anxiety regarding the home, especially towards the end of life. Domestic affairs seem always a source of trouble and difficulty.

The Sun: Indicates success at the end of life, with many desires realized, as well as gain through legacies. If afflicted there will be a tendency to extravagance and exceeding the income, especially towards the close of existence.

The Moon: Shows that chances of inheriting from parents will be uncertain. If afflicted there will be early separation from the parents. It also denotes many changes of residence, help from women and some public recognition if well aspected.

PLANETS IN THE FIFTH HOUSE

Neptune: If afflicted, denotes a chaotic emotional life expressed in an unusual way. When

INFLUENCE OF THE PLANETS

well aspected it brings intuitive associations with the opposite sex which prove helpful in a creative way along artistic lines.

Uranus: Placed in this house love affairs are liable to come to a sudden end and will be chiefly of an illegal type. It is not good for children, who may either die or leave the home at an early age or become estranged if the relationship is sustained longer.

Saturn: Causes frustration in love affairs, either through death or coldness of temperament on either side. If seriously afflicted there may be some physical abnormality reacting upon the emotional life. It is bad for children and risky financial ventures.

Mars: Denotes a reckless emotional nature and disastrous love affairs if afflicted. In any case the emotions are apt to get out of hand and so lead to errors that will be afterwards regretted. Children may be subject to accidents and speculation prove unfortunate.

Venus: Placed here denotes successful love affairs, speculations and happiness through children. Dramatic or musical activities are likely to prove successful if this planet is well aspected.

Mercury: Causes worry connected with love affairs, children and speculation. When afflicting Mars and Uranus there may be some scandal connected with these matters. Mercury is not well placed here as the mind tends to become too much absorbed in the feelings and with the emotional lives of others.

The Sun : Denotes success in connexion with the drama or speculation, especially if well aspected. If afflicted it does not favour the birth of children or speculative matters.

The Moon : Is fortunate for publicity, especially in connexion with the stage. Children should bring happiness and one may become famous. Yet the love affairs are likely to be numerous and the emotional associations ephemeral. If the Moon is afflicted there will be numerous intrigues of short duration which may react disastrously at times, often causing undesirable notoriety.

PLANETS IN THE SIXTH HOUSE

Neptune : Placed here sometimes causes strange psychic diseases difficult to cure. Psychic phenomena would react disastrously upon the health in this case and so should be avoided, even though Neptune be free from affliction. When adversely aspected, there is illness through drugs or debauchery, also treachery amongst employees.

Uranus : Denotes unusual complaints arising from nervous causes. Electricity or osteopathy are the best cures for Uranian sicknesses. If seriously afflicted, epilepsy or hypochondria are likely, and become all but incurable. Servants prove unreliable.

INFLUENCE OF THE PLANETS

Saturn : Illnesses through chills or insufficient nourishment are probable. When the Luminaries afflict Saturn, ill-health is likely to affect the whole life. Servants prove deceitful unless this planet is free from affliction. Often the tastes are fastidious and restrained.

Jupiter : Gives good health ; excess, however, may cause temporary sickness. When this planet is well aspected, in some way gain of a psychological nature is achieved through sickness. Servants prove faithful.

Mars : Indicates untrustworthy servants. The bowels are subject to various disorders and there is the possibility of suffering through inflammatory complaints if afflicted, also through accidents if Mars be placed in a fiery sign.

Venus : Denotes good health, provided excess is avoided. Servants also prove helpful and kindly disposed.

Mercury : Denotes mental troubles or danger of nervous breakdown if afflicted. There is also some danger of chronic dyspepsia. The mind is often interested in the study of herbs and recondite ways of healing.

The Sun : Is not good for health, being considered weak in this house. The heart, especially, may cause trouble.

The Moon : Indicates that the health will be liable to breakdown, especially the digestive sys-

EXOTERIC ASTROLOGY

tem. When afflicting Mars from this house, there is danger of suffering from inflammatory complaints, and when afflicted by Saturn there may be rheumatism.

PLANETS IN THE SEVENTH HOUSE

Neptune: Causes irregular or homosexual attachments both before and after marriage, often leading to scandal if afflicted. Desire is frustrated through some limitation of the partner, either physical or emotional. Women with this position at birth sometimes find themselves deserted at the last moment before marriage.

Uranus: Denotes erratic attachments, an unexpected, sudden marriage followed by separation or divorce within a few years. If afflicted, the wife or business partner may become an open enemy and so cause legal troubles. When well aspected the wife or husband shares the same mental interests and possesses an original mind or strong will.

Saturn: Denotes a faithful but undemonstrative partner if well aspected and a cruel or treacherous one if afflicted. Under the latter conditions marriage is not advisable.

Jupiter: Promises a faithful and fortunate partner, who often possesses wealthy connexions. Marriage may be delayed if this planet is afflicted by Saturn, or there may be legal difficulties if

INFLUENCE OF THE PLANETS

by Mars or Uranus. Yet enemies may become friends under a favourable Solar aspect.

Mars : Is unfortunate for a man, for the wife is apt to become dictatorial even when well aspected and a virago or a drunkard if afflicted. In a woman's nativity this position sometimes causes the husband's death. Mars tending to extremes in all matters, even when free from affliction. Legal matters entail loss.

Venus : Promises a happy union and success after marriage, especially in connexion with social matters. Venus is well placed in this house through her affinity with Libra, the seventh sign ; thus the partner's influence improves the life in every way.

Mercury : Denotes a nervy but clever partner, who is inclined to bickering if afflicted. When well aspected the partner is mentally enterprising. Troubles may occur through correspondence or litigation causing many small worries.

The Sun : Confers happiness through marriage, about middle life. If afflicted, legal difficulties are likely.

The Moon : Indicates a fickle partner. It favours an early marriage and the partner usually desires change and travel. When afflicted, it brings an early death of the partner, sometimes legal difficulties and female enmity.

EXOTERIC ASTROLOGY

PLANETS IN THE EIGHTH HOUSE

Neptune: Gives trouble through dreams, the marriage partner's affairs and through drugs if afflicted. In all these matters conditions will be chaotic and uncertain. There is also some danger of premature burial. When well aspected it denotes benefits through legacies or unexpected ways through others.

Uranus: Denotes that the partner may have trouble through sudden financial disasters. Death may be due to paralysis or a shock of some kind. When well aspected, it brings unexpected legacies and dreams may prove uncommon and often prophetic. There is usually considerable interest in occult matters.

Saturn: Indicates losses after marriage, including the ultimate possession of expected legacies. Death is the result from some long-standing complaint if afflicted, and the life is prolonged when well aspected.

Jupiter: Denotes a peaceful death and gain through the partner or legacies. In some cases the dream consciousness is active and fruitful. When seriously afflicted death is due to consumption, tumours or cancer.

Mars: Causes a sudden or violent death if afflicted. Legacies create legal difficulties and the wife is usually extravagant. If in a watery

INFLUENCE OF THE PLANETS

sign there is danger of drowning, if in an airy one danger by air, and if in a fiery sign danger through fire.

Venus: Denotes a peaceful and easy death, unless afflicted, when there may be kidney troubles. Legacies prove helpful and there should be financial gain through marriage or partnerships, especially after middle life.

Mercury: Causes death through nervous complaints, especially if afflicted by the malefics. There is often financial worry through the partner's deficiency. In the case of a woman, difficulty in obtaining money from the husband. The mind is interested in occult subjects.

The Sun: The life improves after forty when well aspected and there is the possibility of posthumous fame. When afflicted the life is threatened through constitutional weakness or violence. Money may be inherited from the father or from the wife, who is usually fortunate.

The Moon: Denotes death through drowning or in some public place. The mother may leave a legacy when well aspected or die early if afflicted. There is often the latent ability for clear dreaming.[1]

---

[1] Planets well aspected in the eighth house stimulate the dream consciousness, with the exception of Saturn. But these dreams rarely react unfavourably upon the mind in the waking state, and do not affect it beyond a few moments after waking. Planets in the ninth house, however, can give terrible dreams, if afflicted, which often react upon the mind

EXOTERIC ASTROLOGY

Although the fortunes may be unsettled after marriage, the partner may ultimately attain celebrity of some sort.

PLANETS IN THE NINTH HOUSE

Neptune: Gives psychic tendencies to the mind, prophetic dreams and strange forebodings. The mind becomes absorbed with unusual theories or psychic phenomena. This is not a good position for this negative planet unless free from affliction. As the ninth house is that of the Guru or teacher, there is the possibility of coming under the influence of a doubtful Guru, who creates chaos instead of order within the consciousness. There may be also trouble on long journeys or through legal matters; such as fraud by trustees or lawyers.

Uranus: In this position denotes extremes regarding the higher mind: either an intense love of metaphysical matters or the reverse. When afflicted it brings trouble through long journeys, the law or occult matters. In extreme cases the mental concepts appear eccentric or even ridiculous to others.

Saturn: Is not favourable for either long

all day. One man with Neptune con. Moon, opp. Saturn and Uranus from the ninth to the third, although possessing a brilliant brain, nearly went out of his mind through his afflicted house of dreams.

INFLUENCE OF THE PLANETS

journeys, legal affairs or occult matters if afflicted, and can produce mental afflictions in extreme cases. It favours scientific or philosophical studies as opposed to emotional forms of religion or mysticism. When well aspected the mind is ascetic and thoughtful.

Jupiter: Gives strong religious feeling and some ability to foresee the future. There may be some success to do with clerical matters, foreign journeys and legal business. If afflicted there will be a tendency to go to extremes in religious matters.

Mars: Frees the mind from conventional customs and beliefs. Too much so in some cases, for then fanatical impulses will dominate reason. There may be losses abroad or through legal matters. The waking consciousness can become affected by unfavourable dreams. When well aspected to Saturn, the mind is capable of concentrated thought upon abstract subjects.

Venus: Denotes a love of music, art and metaphysical or occult subjects. It promises benefits through long journeys, through shipping and artistic matters. This position is considered to preserve the life from any serious harm.

Mercury: This position gives literary ability, chiefly of a metaphysical type, but unless well aspected to Saturn, the mind lacks the concentration to achieve much in this way. When afflicted there is often a tendency to take on too many activities at one time ; or to hold contradictory opinions about things. In other cases the mind wavers in times of mental crisis. Legal difficulties are also threatened.

The Sun : Denotes success abroad and through established concerns. The mind is apt to be over-confident and impervious to prevailing opinions. When afflicted the whole life may be spoilt through mental narrowness or false pride. There is usually considerable ability to take on responsibility.

The Moon : This position gives many voyages and success abroad. The mind is progressive and eager to learn, but inclined to be superficial or unable to sustain one line of thought for very long. Unless reinforced by positive planets, there will not be much success in matters connected with this house.

PLANETS IN THE TENTH HOUSE

Neptune : Placed here indicates unusual occupations or interests, but if well aspected there may be some success along artistic lines of a bizarre kind, sometimes through assuming another name or personality, for people who respond to this position are apt to be swayed very much by the mood of the moment. When afflicted there is often scandal which ruins the career in some

INFLUENCE OF THE PLANETS

cases. This position creates a strong desire to follow some other profession than the one practised, regardless of whether there is any ability to attain success in that direction.

Uranus: In this house denotes many ups and downs in the career, often involving a complete change of occupation. The mind will be eccentric and keen on original pursuits. Estrangement from friends and relatives is likely. There may be also considerable opposition from public bodies to contend with if afflicted. Sudden success is often balanced by unexpected disaster.[1]

Saturn: Denotes a precarious condition at some time of the life. Yet the elevation of this planet gives great ambition and desire for public esteem as well as perseverance in attaining the goal. If afflicted there is not sufficient ability to realize the individual limitations. There may be a rise, only to fall again through over-estimation of the inherent capabilities. In extreme cases it brings unusual success, followed by dishonour and failure. A fatality hangs over the life from birth.[2]

Jupiter: Brings recognition, prosperity and social benefits if well aspected. If afflicted, legal troubles or reversals of fortune. This position

---
[1] Mussolini had this position at birth.
[2] Napoleon I, Oscar Wilde and Adolph Hitler all had this position at birth.

often indicates good birth or favourable surroundings and social opportunities.

Mars : Is fortunate for the army or the engineering profession. It gives much energy which enables the will to overcome the stormy periods to which the career will be subject. The desires will prove stronger than the mind and so errors in judgment are likely. Similarly there will be a tendency to exhaust the body through over-activity and to live too much in the present.

Venus : This position favours artistic pursuits. Women should prove helpful to the career, which will be aided through a pleasant manner and a kindly disposition. If seriously afflicted there is little scope for creative ability.

Mercury : Gives many interests and a restless mind. There will be a lack of stability, unless reinforced by powerful planets. Success is possible through speaking, writing, contracts, trading or the higher professions. If afflicted the moral standards are sacrificed for mundane success or business deals.

The Sun : This position brings recognition through social matters, government appointments, etc., about middle life. If afflicted there may be too much arrogance and self-assertion, or the position may be obtained and held more through influence than individual ability.

The Moon : Denotes many changes of position

INFLUENCE OF THE PLANETS

with a strong desire to come before the public. Women may assist the career if well aspected or otherwise if afflicted. There is frequently a rise only to be followed by a reversal and scandal. In any case, there is rarely much stability regarding the career.

PLANETS IN THE ELEVENTH HOUSE

Neptune: Denotes strange friendships of a unique kind if favourably aspected. In other cases alliances will prove untrustworthy or even treacherous. When well aspected, intuitive, unusual associations with the opposite sex are possible.

Uranus: Indicates remarkable friendships of a sudden nature are likely to be formed and as quickly broken. Thus magnetic attractions may end in hatred. If afflicted by Mars, Venus or Neptune, homosexual associations will take a similar course.

Saturn: Denotes the existence of deceitful friends, if afflicted, who will prove useless in difficult times. If well aspected, older people may prove helpful, although these associations are few in the life.

Jupiter: Brings friends that are helpful, some of them holding important or influential positions. This being also the house of hopes and wishes, many of the desires in life will be realized. Fortunate aspects made to other planets from this house will considerably reinforce those activities associated with it.

Mars : Denotes few reliable friends but many rackety associations of the " easy-come, easy-go " type. If Mars is afflicted by Neptune in a woman's nativity, the husband's friends will be, like himself, of a dissipated type. If Mars afflicts Uranus, there will be tragic and fateful friendships.

Venus : This position brings gain through friends and fortunate associations. If Venus be in conjunction with Neptune, there will be a remarkable love affair ; if to Uranus, some great fascination for another ; to Saturn, a fatalistic attachment ; and to Mercury, danger of deception.

Mercury : Denotes youthful associations or friendship with scientific or literary people. If afflicted, worry or deception in connexion with friends is possible.

The Sun : Gives stable connexions who hold important positions. These people should prove helpful to the career and bring about some of the hopes and wishes. Success after middle life is likely if the Sun be free from affliction.

The Moon : Indicates that friends are usually unreliable and acquaintances of a superficial character. There is the power to make immediate adaptations to others, although the contact is

INFLUENCE OF THE PLANETS

hardly likely to last. There are often several children in the family, who influence the life in a marked way.

PLANETS IN THE TWELFTH HOUSE

Neptune: Denotes many secret enemies if afflicted. If well aspected benefits are likely through secret or occult associations unsuspected by others.

Uranus: Brings unexpected difficulties through others, who create an antagonistic attitude within the family circle. If in conjunction with the Moon, there may be several love affairs of a secret nature, which all end abruptly after a brief tense period of mutual interest. It favours secret work or occult research.

Saturn: Indicates secret enemies who prove unrelenting throughout the life if afflicted. This position only favours those who seek seclusion, and then this planet must be well aspected or the mind may become morbid, especially if Mercury afflicts Saturn.

Jupiter: Promises success in occult pursuits or welfare work. Enemies sometimes become friends if well aspected. There are also dual love affairs or two interests which influence the life.

Mars: Shows danger of confinement or treachery of a political or an emotional nature. It is bad for psychic work and there is danger through animals.

Venus: Indicates that secret love affairs will lead to jealousy or trouble of some kind if afflicted. If well aspected these relationships will escape the notice of others. This position often causes an early marriage but brings another influence into the life which may lead to a divorce.

Mercury: Denotes a subtle mind with a taste for mysterious mental pursuits of a somewhat risky nature, provided it is well aspected. If afflicted, self-esteem or assurance is lacking.

The Sun: Causes estrangement from kindred, the mind has occult interests which are not shared by the family. If well aspected the conditions improve through individual effort after one-third of the life is past.

The Moon: Indicates emotional frustration or enforced physical confinement if afflicted. If well aspected there is considerable interest in occult pursuits. The disposition is lacking in firmness and so easily open to the influence of others, especially the opposite sex. Love affairs are apt to be indiscreet, often causing financial loss thereby.

CHAPTER IX

HEALTH AND THE HYLEG

THE Hyleg is that point in the horoscope upon which health and life depend, requiring careful consideration when estimating the probable length of life and the strength of the body. According to some astrologers, the hyleg is not concerned with health so much as longevity. Furthermore, opinions vary as to the right way of selecting the hyleg. Some insist that the Sun is always hyleg; others think the Sun for men and the Moon for women.

According to Claudius Ptolemy, the father of Western astrology, the following houses are " hylegiacal ", the first, the seventh, the ninth, and tenth houses and that half of the eleventh house nearest the M.C. If the Sun is therein, it is hyleg; if it is not, but the Moon is, she is hyleg; if neither is, the ascendant is considered. An orb of five degrees above the cusp of the ascendant and twenty-five below would be the limits of reckoning, whilst the Western angle would count from five degrees below to twenty-five above. The remaining houses are unimportant, for they could not be hyleg. The two luminaries and the ascendant must be considered regarding the length of life. If the ascendant is negative, it absorbs the influence of the Moon and its aspects; if it be positive, then the Sun and its aspects must be considered.

The luminaries in benefic aspect to the ascendant insure a sound body. On the other hand, bad aspects to that point or the luminaries menace the life. Favourable and afflicting aspects to the ascendant must be weighed up to form a correct judgment of health.

If all three influences are well aspected, a healthy and long life can be expected. If any of the three are afflicted, especially if the afflicting influence rules the fourth, eighth or twelfth houses or is placed therein, ill-health relative to that particular influence and the sign it contains, is liable to menace the life, according to the type of affliction.

The degree upon the cusp of the ascendant must be considered equal in importance to that of the luminaries, and aspects should be calculated to it from all the planets.

The positive or odd signs rising give vitality, particularly Aries, Leo and Sagittarius; the negative signs are not so strong, Cancer and Pisces being particularly weak, especially in infancy.

HEALTH AND THE HYLEG

Scorpio gives considerable energy, but there is some liability to infectious diseases.

The Sun is considered the most important influence in a man's nativity and the Moon in a woman's. The Moon rules both sexes in early life.

A malefic exactly upon the fourth or seventh house cusp when afflicting the Sun, Moon or ascendant is a frequent cause of children dying at birth. Similarly, if the Moon be in conjunction with the Sun and not reinforced by a trine to Jupiter, there is an early death. Especially if both luminaries receive a bad aspect from a malefic.

HEALING AND THE NEW AGE

Each Age requires its particular method of healing. Two thousand years ago, Christ inaugurated a method of healing suited to the emotional sign Pisces, and so His cures were chiefly affected by the readjustment of the sympathetic system through an appeal made to the higher emotions. At that time the mind was not sufficiently advanced to be much influenced one way or the other.

In the Coming Age, under Aquarius, a mental airy sign, the diseases will be largely the result of maladjustment between the conscious and unconscious minds or a mental inability to keep

EXOTERIC ASTROLOGY

pace with the rush and ruthlessness of modern life.[1] The modern mind is not open, as a rule, to an emotional appeal that presupposes a belief in transcendentalism, unless there is a strong watery influence in the nativity. The intelligentsia demand expert, individual psychological assistance in most cases. The influence of Saturn, ruler of Aquarius, will slowly supersede Jupiter, ruler of Pisces. Nevertheless, many people, chiefly functioning in the sympathetic system, which dominated the Pisces Age, are still benefited through group invocation as seen at Lourdes and at other Christian gatherings.

Psycho-analysis is therefore a sign of the times. Whilst yet in its infancy, the method remains intensely Saturnian. Later on a Uranian method will be evolved. In this the patient will take over the full control of the unconscious mind through the will. Thus whilst the Christian Era encouraged placing our burdens upon Christ, the Aquarian method will instruct each man how to bear his own load in the centuries to come.

CURES EFFECTED THROUGH DIET

Whilst nervous complaints are distinctly Aquarian and are usually the result of mental-emotional

[1] In this connexion the reader may find much of interest in *Oracle*, a novel by Lucian Wainwright (Methuen, Ltd.). Although in the guise of fiction, it presents a true picture of *pioneer* efforts at healing along the new Aquarian lines.

HEALTH AND THE HYLEG

disturbance or maladjustment, other modern diseases such as Cancer (now enormously on the increase) are the result of etheric dislocation. There are three methods of cure : through operations, inoculation and diet. The first involves Mars or the knife skilfully applied ; the second Neptune or drugs, with equally doubtful results ; and the third Saturnian, which is characteristically based upon doing *without* certain things, chiefly meat. This method is still in the experimental stage.[1]

Perhaps never before in history has diet played such an important part in our daily lives or been so universally studied by specialists of all kinds in their sustained endeavour to cure ailing humanity. Saturnian restrictions play an increasingly important part in the daily life of the wealthy or moderately well-to-do. Our forefathers of " the roast beef of old England " type would be appalled and dismayed if called upon to live chiefly on raw salads and fruit.[2]

It is a distinctly ironical fact that there has been far more response to vegetarianism purely for health reasons, than to the simple humanitarian

[1] Those countries which have the highest consumption of meat per head of the population, also have the highest deathrate from Cancer. The strict vegetarian is less likely to suffer from Cancer than the eater of flesh food.

[2] Yet there are people born with Virgo rising or afflicted, who cannot digest a diet consisting of raw or even cooked vegetables. If they do so the result is colitis.

appeal, "Stop eating meat because of the cruelty to animals". That this should be so is another expression of the cold, self-centred side of Saturn.[1]

[1] For readers interested in the modern problem of Healing and the New Age, there is much of value and interest in *Doctors, Disease and Health*, by Cyril Scott (Methuen).

CHAPTER X

TRANSITS

A TRANSIT is the temporary passage of a planet over a sensitive point in the radical horoscope. These influences must be taken from the ephemeris of the current year. Raphael has published a table of planetary places of Neptune, Uranus, Jupiter, Saturn and Mars with their declinations from the first of each month from 1900 to 2001 (price 1s.).

A slow-moving planet is far more potent when operating as a transit than a quick one, such as Mercury. Venus also may be disregarded, owing to its speed, when considered in this way. Transits are most effective when they act as re-vitalizing forces with regard to a radical aspect or sensitive point.

For instance, if the Sun is five degrees Scorpio and is in trine to Uranus in five degrees Pisces, then any transit of the Sun or Uranus over any point in aspect with five degrees Scorpio or five degrees Pisces will re-vitalize the radical aspect. A transit of any other planet, except the above, would not act in such a forceful way.

Each planet will colour each house with its characteristic influence when operating as a transit, and would be particularly strong if aspecting the ruler or occupant of the house in question of the radical chart. In a general sense the slower-moving planets have the greatest influence and last the longest time.

Neptune causes conflicting conditions, delays or treachery if afflicted and beneficial surprises if well aspected.

Uranus invariably brings the unexpected, often involving drastic changes. These would be good or bad according to the aspects formed.

Saturn, if well aspected, gives favourable conditions of a consolidating type, and loss, opposition or an involved state of affairs if afflicted.

Jupiter alternates between stimulating good fortune or causing waste and extravagance according to the aspects. In occult houses its influence would operate chiefly as a spiritual stimulus. As a rule, Jupiter produces expansion as opposed to the contraction associated with Saturn (unless very well aspected).

In a general sense the influence of Mars resembles that of Uranus, for both hasten events according to the influence of the house containing them.

The quicker planets do not remain sufficiently long in one house to stimulate its influence very much one way or the other.

TRANSITS

Saturn takes twenty-eight years to complete the circle of the Zodiac; Jupiter takes twelve years; Mars about two years and Uranus about eighty-four years.

Transits over the radical Sun, Moon, ascendant or mid-heaven, or, to a lesser extent, the progressed Sun and Moon, can have a distinct influence upon current conditions. Nevertheless, transits are subsidiary to progressed aspects (secondary directions) and so should not be over-stressed when receiving consideration. Considerable intuition is needed to gauge the approximate influence of a transit with regard to present events.

THE PROGRESSED HOROSCOPE

There are various ways of progressing a horoscope, but here only the SECONDARY progressions will be considered, being the simplest and most generally used to-day. The technique is not complicated and can be applied to the ordinary ephemeris for the birth year. Secondary progressions are calculated with regard to the apparent motion of the Sun and the Solar day—counting from noon to noon. Thus a Solar day becomes a Solar year. Should you wish to know what is likely to occur about your thirtieth birthday, then count thirty days after that date and fill in the progressed position of the planets in a different-coloured ink, which facilitates distinguishing between the radical and progressed positions of the planets. This is a useful custom, especially amongst beginners.

It will be found that whilst Mercury, Venus and Mars will have moved considerably in that period, the slower planets will have remained much where they were, especially if any happen to be retrograde. The Moon takes about twenty-eight years to again reach its radical position.

In a mundane way the progressing of the Moon is a very important factor, if applied to the radical chart, especially when in the vicinity of the mid-heaven or the ascendant. In the first case improved mundane conditions are likely, and in the second a physical change in the surroundings or occupation is frequent, although not inevitable.

PROGRESSING THE ASCENDANT

Progressed aspects to radical positions are usually far more pronounced than progressed aspects to the progressed chart. To explain this in greater detail, it will be found that if you progress a nativity for thirty years hence at exactly the same time as the birth moment, another sign will be ruling the ascendant. Some astrologers will consider this new ascendant of great importance.

I have discussed this point with other astrolo-

TRANSITS

gers and have come to the same conclusion as they have—namely, that the progressed ascendant has very little influence upon the life, although the progressed planets have a great deal. This conclusion would seem to be borne out by the fact that our appearance changes but little, certainly it never takes on the physical or mental characteristics of the signs that follow in succession, according to how long the life lasts. But it is obvious to a discriminating person how some of us change according to our progressed aspects. For instance, a man born under a placid configuration, consisting of numerous trines and sextiles, gradually or suddenly appears to his friends as nervous or irritable as the trines and sextile aspects become automatically squares or oppositions with the passing of time. Similarly, those born irritable or frustrated will cease to be so when they progress out of the bad aspects into favourable combinations of planets and signs.

To be born with a lucky spoon in one's mouth does not guarantee that favourable conditions will remain fixed indefinitely, otherwise the will would not develop. Hence the significance and importance of progressing the horoscope and of making our plans accordingly.

For instance, I was asked to progress the horoscope of a successful theatrical producer, who had been very fortunate with a play which ran over a year in London, and later became equally popular on tour and as a film. This man's benefic progressed *Jupiter-Venus* aspect, like many others, only lasted about two years. I warned him not to launch out any further, as he was about to experience all the limitations and frustrations of progressed *Saturn* square radical *Moon*. Unfortunately his belief in astrology was not sufficient to induce him to close down his offices and numerous subsidiary activities for the three years involved. The result was he lost all and even more than he had previously made through further artistic productions, under the baleful *Saturn* progressed aspect.

Now that the science of astrology is being more recognized in America, big business men pay large fees to experienced astrologers to ascertain fortunate periods for speculative or other ventures. It may be that if film stars are progressing through bad periods, which are likely to last indefinitely, they are not " signed on " in certain cases. The progressed aspects of future actors will be as carefully considered as the existing reports sent in regarding their films from the cinema box offices all over the country.

This is somewhat *Saturnian* and ruthless, but no more so than a doctor's unfavourable report regarding a noted boxer. Forewarned is forearmed, and if film stars accepted astrology, they would respond to *Saturn* and husband their resources when under good aspects, realizing that these could not last for very long.

In a book of this nature it is impossible to go into great detail regarding the progressed horoscope, which involves primary, secondary and radix directions. Astrologers differ here—as in many other ways—with regard not only to their various significance and importance, but also which type is the most effective.[1]

But in all cases the radical planets seem to become vitalized as progressed planets form a close aspect with them. Yet to build too much upon benefic progressed aspects is an error if the radical chart indicates lack of opportunity, will-power or initiative.

The most fateful nativities are those in which the majority of the planets are in mutable signs or where Saturn afflicts the Sun and Moon, or the malefics Mars and Uranus afflict each other, the

[1] The most difficult and least understood part of astrology is the *Directional*, or the calculation of future events. There are Zodiacal directions, Mundane directions, Secondary directions, progressed cusps, Revolutionary figures, Eclipses, New Moons, etc., etc., until, in short, if they were all calculated in detail, there would be at least an important influence every week on an average. The stern facts of life do not bear out such copious influences, and it is practically *a waste of time* to work out the Primaries, as they are called, when not more than 10 per cent. will be found to coincide with an event. . . . The Secondary as taught in my " key " comes nearer to the truth than any, yet it is sadly deficient and unreliable. —Raphael's *Ephemeris*.

EXOTERIC ASTROLOGY

Sun or Saturn. Nevertheless, progressed aspects indicate tendencies or mundane possibilities which should not be ignored by the student.

ECLIPSES

These influence the nativity in much the same way as a powerful conjunction, beneficial or otherwise. As has been said earlier in this book, if a Solar eclipse forms a close adverse aspect to a vital planet or the ascendant in the radical chart, it may cause death. But this possibility may not occur immediately and may also be counteracted altogether by benefics reinforcing the configuration affected. If the eclipse falls within the eleventh house of hopes and wishes, then some sudden disappointment may be the result, should it form a bad aspect to some other planet in the radical chart. Wherever it forms, that that particular house will be affected adversely goes without saying, unless considerably counteracted by benefics.

Whilst agreeing with Raphael's dictum regarding the possible confusion of elaborate directions and numerous calculations, I still feel that *secondary* directions can give excellent results, for I have proved them. Similarly, a study of transits can also prove very helpful regarding a particular problem. The main thing to remember is the importance of the radical figure, however it is

TRANSITS

applied. That is to say, concentrate upon progressed planets *only* with regard to the radical figure. Likewise carefully consider the radical chart with relation to the transits.

CHAPTER XI

THE ART OF SYNTHESIS

IT is not the purpose of this book to explore ground already ably covered by numerous astrologers, but rather to suggest how the sixth sense in astrology can be developed by the more intuitive type of mind.

Such people do not have to be convinced as to the truth of this science, yet they are not usually experts at making or using logarithms, in addition to the involved calculations that are easily comprehended by the purely mathematical mind.

The Indian method of casting the figure and then concentrating in meditation only upon the diagram for some hours before attempting a delineation has much to recommend it. By this means, to the intuitive, the nativity yields up its secrets. When intuition is lacking, the whole figure may appear a hopeless jumble of conflicting forces, which appear to the astrologer as almost equally powerful.

Nevertheless, there are some general hints which can always be followed by even the most inex-

THE ART OF SYNTHESIS

perienced student. These suggestions have never, as far as I know, been put forward as astrological axioms in a succinct manner. It is the main purpose of this book to stress these points for the sake of the beginner who wishes to grasp the essentials before he becomes lost in a maze of intricate details.

An important point to consider is the position of the planets. If they are rising (third, second, first, twelfth, eleventh and tenth houses), there is the most scope for individual expression or success in the world, particularly if several are in the tenth house or mid-heaven. If the majority of the planets are setting (ninth, eighth, seventh, sixth, fifth and fourth houses), there is less scope for success and the career is dependent largely upon the help of others. Should the majority of the planets be below the horizon (first, second, third, fourth, fifth and sixth), there is not much success until the end of life, and then only if the planets are well aspected.

These combinations will be seen at a glance. Further consideration will be needed regarding the aspects the planets form first in relation to the houses and then with regard to each other.

Attention must then be directed to the position of the Sun and Moon. If the Sun be above the horizon (twelfth, eleventh, tenth, ninth, eighth and seventh), the ego or higher self has an opportunity in this life to control the emotions to a certain extent. It can also achieve some of the inner desires, according to the strength of its house, sign and aspects. If, however, the Sun is weak, below the horizon, and the Moon is above it, strongly aspected and favourably placed, then the personality—consisting of ephemeral desires and ambitions—will dominate the ego or higher self in most cases, and so the whole life will become subject to the mood of the moment. It is not too much to say that, unless the Sun is well placed and aspected in the fourth house, it will have but little influence upon the life if in other houses below the horizon at birth.

There are certain exceptions, however, such as the *Sun* rising in the first house in a fiery sign. This combination should influence the body towards idealistic action, especially when in conjunction with the *Moon*. If the *Moon* be in the vicinity of the tenth house, then the personal desires or ambitions would be likely to prove too strong to be controlled. When the rising Sun is in the twelfth house, there should be an inner power to weigh up passing moods or desires with an ability to overcome them through a process of mental self-questioning, which ruthlessly subjects all things to a dispassionate analysis.

After the ascendant, the position of the planets and their reactions to the Luminaries have been

THE ART OF SYNTHESIS

co-related, there remain the houses containing the majority of the planets.

Through casting and delineating numerous horoscopes I have discovered that the houses containing the planets are the most important ones to consider. The consciousness is chiefly focused there, for the activities of these houses will be largely coloured by the characteristics of the planets involved. Those houses without planets may be considered negligible. The usual procedure, however, is to consider the position and aspects of the planet ruling the sign upon its cusp and requires considerable experience to gauge correctly.

Sometimes the planets are spread over a wide field, perhaps one in each house. In nativities such as these, several benefic aspects are frequently formed, and so the life runs in pleasant places and the disposition is frequently versatile, charming and fortunate, but lacks mundane difficulties to overcome. The horoscope of the Duke of Windsor is one of this type. Other charts contain several planets placed in one house, perhaps in opposition to others. These aspects create both inner tension and external conflict for the individual concerned but also denote much internal strength, which can become harmonized through self-conscious effort. The first thing to concentrate upon in such a case is the particular characteristics of the houses affected by the opposition.

EXOTERIC ASTROLOGY

For instance, if the planets afflict each other from the third to the ninth houses, there is considerable difficulty in harmonizing the lower concrete mind with the abstract subjective mind. Moreover, such an individual can receive but little help from others regarding this particular problem. Either the lower mind dominates the higher and so a somewhat materialistic point of view is cultivated regarding all higher thought, or else a subjective attitude towards life is adopted to the extent of completely ignoring everyday problems. J. Krishnamurti's nativity is one of the latter type.

Another example of several planets in opposition to each other is the nativity of the late Annie Besant, only in her case the first and seventh houses were chiefly involved. Thus her mundane activities required a series of partners or co-workers who sometimes became open enemies to the extent of involving her in litigation. As in her case, both the first and seventh house planets afflicted *Jupiter* and the *Moon* in her fourth; the end of her life was rather a sad one. At her death many problems, involving her relationships with others, were still unsolved.

These examples are stated with a view to comparison.[1] The Western astrologer is only capable

---

[1] The late Annie Besant was the last great initiate of the expiring Pisces cycle. But she was too much of an extravert

THE ART OF SYNTHESIS

of arriving at truth through such means. Assuming that a certain configuration proves true in the past with well-known or historic people (whose nativities are already published), a similar configuration in any other horoscope will presage similar events. If in a number of instances similar results are obtained, astrological delineations will carry far more weight with the average Western mind.

When the oppositions and square aspects have been considered with regard to their house positions, it would be also as well to consider their respective elements. Should they be from fire to air, as in the case of Annie Besant, then idealistic action and mental conflict or attempted co-operation with others will be the source of tension. If the affliction is from earth to water—involving the third and ninth houses—as with J. Krishnamurti,

to realize the full significance of this fact. An *external* Venusian-Martian occult stimulus became expressed through her angular planets in *cardinal* signs. This stellar permutation can never be repeated, for it created an etheric vacuum skilfully attuned to the passing Age. Therefore a repolarization from *fixed* signs was the *karmic* aftermath, through the extreme introversion of her *Aquarian* successor, J. Krishnamurti. The law of action and reaction applies to occult activities as well as to others. Probably her next nativity will express planets in fixed rather than cardinal signs, although these may be rising. The nativities of the late Annie Besant and J. Krishnamurti are published in *Adepts of the Five Elements*, in relation to that of the Theosophical Society, as alternate expressions of extraverted and introverted stimuli respectively.

EXOTERIC ASTROLOGY

the earth is ignored so that a detached sublimated attitude of mind is imposed upon an emotional or watery medium, because the opposition occurs from *mental* houses : a contradiction in astrological terms creating considerable inner tension.

Looked at in this way, the prevailing influence of the life can be seen through *one* important aspect. Of course, there are also other subordinate influences of lesser importance but of equal interest. Such as Neptune, without aspects, in the fourth house, the end of life, in the nativity of J. Krishnamurti.

In any case, it is always well to look to the fourth house in every horoscope, for it contains not only a prediction with regard to the end of life but also indicates how everything else is likely to turn out in the end.

To simplify this attempt at astrological synthesis, it is well to stress the need of separating the objective or active side of a nativity from the subjective. Planets in the first, second, third, fifth, seventh, tenth and eleventh houses give scope for practical or active ways of living. On the other hand, planets in the fourth, eighth, ninth and twelfth houses operate subjectively and turn the consciousness inward in search of realities, chiefly through various psychic interests. Planets in the eighth house bring illumination through dreams, and in the ninth house both dreams and

THE ART OF SYNTHESIS

waking visions or mental intuitions of an illuminating nature. Planets in the twelfth and fourth houses cause a voluntary retirement from mundane activities, in order that the individual may attain spiritual experience and realization of a psychic nature through his own efforts.

SOME OPPOSING OR COMPLEMENTARY HOUSES

In studying the influence of the mind upon the nativity, the third and ninth houses are considered. The personal emotional desires and their more sublimated form of platonic friendship are associated with the fifth and its opposite the eleventh house. It may be noted here that the two houses *above* the horizon, the ninth and the eleventh, indicate the higher aspect of consciousness in both the mind and the emotions.

Those people born with a strong fifth house have always to contend with powerful desires throughout the life. Frequently these become expressed through personal emotions, such as acting or singing, leading to popularity or notoriety according to whether the aspects are favourable or otherwise. Several planets in the eleventh house become expressed through the comparatively impersonal associations to be found upon boards, committees and other public bodies. On the other hand, those unions confined to a powerful fifth house, containing several planets, are intense whilst they last, but are apt to break up when afflicted from mundane or mental houses (planets in the third or the ninth usually).

Afflictions from the second to the eighth house cause loss of money or legacies through the machinations of others : from the fourth to the tenth, some error connected with the career reacts unfavourably upon the home or vice versa : from the twelfth to the sixth, psychic effort, sustained unwisely or under adverse surroundings, reacts upon the health.

People born with many planets in either the twelfth or the sixth houses or both are usually frustrated in mundane matters and so forced to become introspective. If these houses contain planets favourably aspected, this introspection may lead to inner psychic development. When these houses are afflicted, the will must be very strong or the mind and the emotions may become warped or repressed according to the planets and signs involved.

The seventh house invariably indicates the strong influence of co-workers upon the whole life. Planets placed here usually bring different types of partners into the life in quick succession, often involving specialized co-operation in public work.[1]

[1] Annie Besant, Hitler and Mussolini, all had powerful planets in the seventh house at birth.

THE ART OF SYNTHESIS

Nevertheless, a man who has planets in his seventh house finds partnership of some sort essential for his well-being. He who has none there is often independent of others. Sometimes he may even feel subtly handicapped if closely associated with anyone else in a physical sense. The seventh house is complementary to the first and indicates the subjective side of the nature as opposed to the objective.

THE MIND AND THE EMOTIONS

All things to do with the mind are under the rulership of *Mercury* if it be in mental houses. Should, however, *Mercury* be placed in a non-mental house, then the planets in the third or ninth house should be considered. If there are no planets in these houses, the rulers of the signs upon their cusp will be related to the mind in a *negative* way.

Similarly when *Mercury* is favourably aspected by other planets the mind is enriched thereby. On the other hand, the thinking process will be hampered according to the affliction which *Mercury* receives.

For instance, *Mercury* trine *Saturn* steadies the mind, giving it sobriety and judgment; *Mercury* afflicted by *Uranus* indicates that the mind will be subject to sudden and erratic errors; *Mercury* in benefic aspect to *Venus* causes the intellectual faculties to be artistic ; *Mercury* in conjunction with *Mars* makes the mind energetic or sarcastic. *Mercury* in conjunction with *Neptune* the mental consciousness will be mystically inclined, if the aspect is unfavourable the mind becomes chaotic or unscrupulous.

The higher emotions are ruled by *Venus*, and the lower desires by *Mars*. Should these afflict each other, there will be great difficulty in harmonizing the influence of these two planets throughout the life. It is not too much to say that the individual concerned will be apt to run amuck especially when under adverse progressed aspects. On the other hand, should these planets be in benefic aspect to *Saturn*, there will be the inner power to control the emotions, a faculty brought over from past lives according to Indian astrologers. Similarly, should *Mars* and *Venus* be in conjunction with *Mercury*, there will be the latent ability to analyse every sensation, even whilst under its influence. The *Venus-Mercury* conjunction would tend to analyse the higher emotions. The *Mars-Mercury* combination would concentrate more upon physical personal desires.

Astrologers have discovered that homosexuality is frequently accompanied by a conjunction of *Neptune* with the *Sun*, *Mars* or the *Moon*, also *Uranus* with *Venus*. Thus with the increasing influence of these far-off planets upon our earth,

THE ART OF SYNTHESIS

homosexuality has also become stimulated considerably. When these planets are favourably aspected, there is often the power to sublimate these tendencies. When afflicted, however, desire is considerably increased and so difficult to control. Should *Uranus* and *Neptune* be placed in mental houses, the potential danger of emotional wreckage is alleviated.

The remaining planets, *Jupiter* and *Saturn*, bring blessings or cause limitations of a purely mundane nature. These planets will act as expanding or contracting influences according to their house positions.

Saturn beneficially aspected is the chief restraining influence in a moral sense, and when *Saturn* is weakly placed and *without* aspects, the moral sense is frequently non-existent.[1] The *Sun* without aspects also indicates lack of morality and often weakness of will. Similarly a weak *Mars* indicates lack of initiative ; an unaspected *Venus* inability to respond to higher emotions associated with music and art, etc. Put briefly, if a planet has no aspects its power to influence the nativity is short-circuited or rendered void.

Exceptionally original minds respond to *Uranus*. These people are usually pioneers or inventors,

[1] A woman, whose nativity had a weak unaspected *Saturn*, was totally without moral sense. Two men, without aspects to the *Sun* at birth, temporarily went out of their minds soon after joining their respective units in the firing line in 1917.

EXOTERIC ASTROLOGY

whilst artists, poets, musicians and mystics respond to the higher side of *Neptune*.

Since 1910, when the opposition between these two mysterious planets was formed, their influence has become increasingly apparent all over the world. According to Indian astrologers, this opposition has made correct prophecies based upon the influence of *Jupiter* and *Venus*, the recognized benefics, almost negligible.

Uranus and *Neptune* will be forming a benefic trine aspect from the earthy signs *Taurus* and *Virgo* between 1938 and 1941. This will be a period fraught with unusual possibilities physically, emotionally and mentally.

CHAPTER XII

WAGNER'S NATIVITY

A BRIEF DELINEATION

THE signs, houses, planets and their aspects have now been dealt with separately and in a general way. Thus having covered the ground, it might be as well to take an example horoscope considering the salient points. In our chart we have Wagner's horoscope cast for sunrise, 22nd May, 1813.

This is a fairly evenly balanced map, since it shows scope both for subjective and objective development, without which no artist can achieve success. It contains three influences just above the horizon in the twelfth house. The first one, closest to the cusp of the ascendant *Gemini*, is the *Sun*, which colours the physical body with all its fire and vitality.

The effect of these three influences [1] in the

---

[1] Some astrologers would consider that the Sun and Venus were so close to the cusp of the ascendant as to operate entirely through the first house. But his secret love affairs, exile and frustration indicate their strong twelfth-house influence. See Sepharial's *Manual of Astrology*, p. 47.

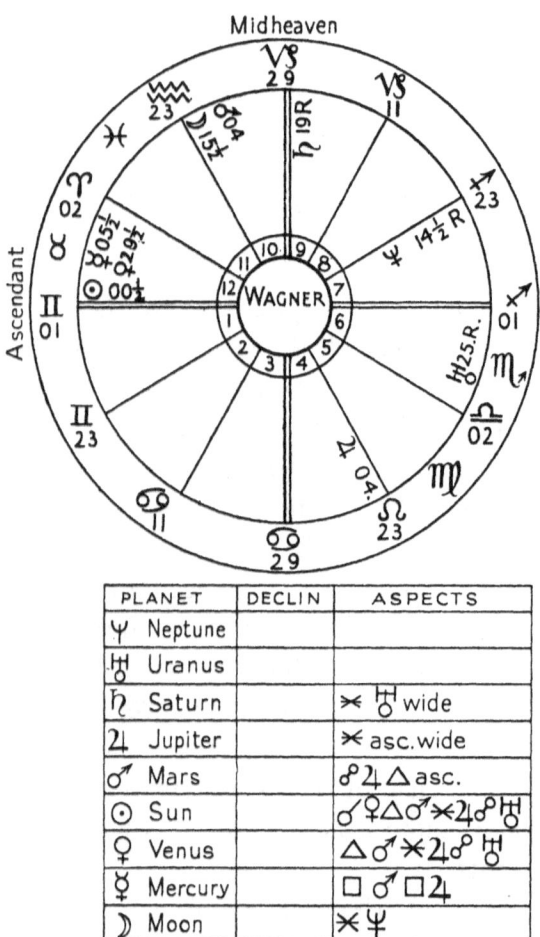

PLANET	DECLIN	ASPECTS
♆ Neptune		
♅ Uranus		
♄ Saturn		⚹ ♅ wide
♃ Jupiter		⚹ asc. wide
♂ Mars		☍ ♃ △ asc.
☉ Sun		☌ ♀ △ ♂ ⚹ ♃ ☍ ♅
♀ Venus		△ ♂ ⚹ ♃ ☍ ♅
☿ Mercury		□ ♂ □ ♃
☽ Moon		⚹ ♆

WAGNER'S NATIVITY

twelfth house, on Wagner's early life, was to force the composer ceaselessly to seek within himself the inner meaning of things. Like all people suffering under a sense of frustration, he was always fighting about something. These incessant conflicts soon involved him in political controversies, and history records his exile on account of his fiery political views. Had the *Sun* been in the tenth house, such experiences would have been unnecessary, and he would have obtained early opportunities for self-expression and recognition such as were afforded Napoleon, Bismarck, Swinburne, and Backhaus, who had this position at birth.

The twelfth house has always been associated with clandestine love affairs, frequently involving a strong attachment which will escape the notice of others (*provided* the planets therein are well aspected). Wagner, having *Venus* placed here, was able to experience every emotion to the uttermost, not only at the time, but afterwards in retrospect through creating his compositions. His affair with Mathilda Wesendonck in Switzerland ultimately led to yet another enforced exile in Venice, where he made his greatest effort towards sublimation by composing *Tristan*.

Mercury, also in this house, gave him a peculiarly subtle mind, one loving risks and dangerous adventures of a secret nature. This position gives undoubted ability, which, however, in his case was always being frustrated. The square aspects to *Mars* and *Jupiter* operating from this house made him ungrateful, prodigal, unfaithful and ruthless, especially where his own desires or ambitions were concerned.

The *Sun* in the twelfth house usually denotes that one-third, if not more, of the life will be spent in obscurity, but through pain and the release of his inhibitions the man may ultimately achieve success. In this case, the benefic sextile to *Jupiter* ensured help, forcing those holding important positions, such as the King of Bavaria, to come to his succour. Ultimate fame and world recognition (*Jupiter* ruling the fourth house) also came through this good aspect.

The next house to contain a planet (for all houses containing no planets are weak as a rule) is the fourth, the maternal and subjective house that rules the end of life. Here we have *Jupiter*, the benefic influence in every horoscope, receiving the benefic sextile aspect from the *Sun*. This combination denotes wealth and prosperity at the end of life. It usually gives a happy home, whilst enterprises turn out favourably. It also shows Wagner's somewhat conventional point of view, doubtless acquired through contact with his second wife, who was far more materially minded and wholly incapable of sustaining his earlier line of inspiration. Had *Uranus*, the erratic and un-

WAGNER'S NATIVITY

conventional influence in every horoscope, been placed here, the end would have been very different.

Uranus, however, was placed in the sixth house, the house of service and sickness; it was also throwing its force into the seventh house of partners, being but a few degrees from its cusp. Those who have this position at birth frequently elect to become servants of humanity, *provided they can do it in their own way*. There is always something of the abnormal latent in this combination, and it often indicates danger of hypochondria and hallucination. Fortunately he was able to absorb the force of the opposition of *Uranus* to the *Sun* on the ascendant and influence not only his contemporaries thereby, but the future generations as well. This aspect caused many obstacles, however, as well as enmities and estrangements, including the inevitable divorce which is often a concomitant of *Uranus* in the neighbourhood of the seventh house, Napoleon's divorce being another case in point.

Neptune, also being in the seventh house, is another strange influence, denoting extremes of fortune and misfortune, as well as extraordinary unions. The seventh house being a subjective one and ruled by the two most subjective planets, Wagner's spiritual aspirations obviously became coloured by them, taking on all the stormy conflict of *Uranus*, as well as the intense desire to yield up everything for some higher ideal which comes through a well-aspected *Neptune*.

All the later period (except the *actual* end of the life) came under the above influences, almost wholly inspiring Wagner's best work. The wide sextile from *Uranus* to *Saturn* in the ninth house, the house of the higher mind, however, gave that austere element to his writing which bordered at times on the sanctimonious, a tendency which increased with years and entirely dominated his last work, *Parsifal*.

Finally, we come to the mid-heaven containing both *Saturn* and *Mars*, and showing a distinct element of conflict in consequence. The first part of the life was energized by the activity and passion of *Mars*, the latter dominated by the austerity associated with the former planet. *Mars* in the tenth house denotes an ambitious and masterful spirit, and is favourable to success in spite of the stormy periods that inevitably arise for all those who have this position at birth. At times the animal and passionate side of the nature is likely to dominate the intellectual, feeling being much stronger than reason, especially during the earlier part of life. Scandal usually accompanies this position, and the close opposition to Jupiter was responsible for Wagner's frequent conflicts with contemporary authorities, in a political as well as in a musical sense. This aspect also makes

WAGNER'S NATIVITY

all those who have it at birth, improvident, over-enthusiastic, and *above all, self-deceptive*. All his gods were Wagners in disguise.

The *Moon* in the mid-heaven denotes fame and publicity and fluctuating success, again with the tendency to suffer through scandal. Fortunately, the *Moon* was free from affliction, and so Wagner was able to live down more than once both disrepute and opposition alike. The fact that the *Moon* was in the sign *Aquarius* considerably increased the tendency indicated elsewhere to mysticism and the occult generally. The *Moon* being above the *Sun* stressed the personal side of life at the expense of the Solar or more selfless element. It would have been difficult for him to have given any other contemporary composer his due, and he would always have fought hard to maintain his position so laboriously acquired.

This nativity is one of those indicating the great importance of planets angular and upon the cusp between two houses. They would not be there unless for a purpose, which is to react upon a wider field of activity than if placed well within one house. Wagner's life undoubtedly expressed both the early frustration, imprisonment and shattering secret love affairs, associated with the Sun and Venus in the twelfth house, combined with the first house Venusian successful expression achieved largely through the Solar will. This combination was reinforced by their mutual benefic aspect to Jupiter, ruling the end of life. Without this combination he might have remained for ever frustrated, especially as Jupiter was in affliction to both Mercury and Mars. Fortunately Mars and the Moon were placed in the tenth house, and so gave force to the powerful desires for personal success.

Had Jupiter or Mars been retrograde, the force associated with their characteristics and house position would have been introverted and he might never have attained the desired goal.

MUNDANE AND PSYCHOLOGICAL EFFECTS OF RETROGRADE PLANETS

As the Solar system is seen from the earth from a slightly peripherical point and not from the centre, the other planets of our system appear to move in an irregular way. Sometimes they seem to remain stationary, at others to move backward in a course opposite to their normal one around the Sun. In the first case they are said to be stationary, in the second retrograde.

In a mundane sense a retrograde planet is considered unfortunate, considerably frustrating the full promise of any favourable aspects it may receive from the luminaries or other planets. In a psychological sense these geocentric traits of the planets are now considered of great importance

WAGNER'S NATIVITY

by a new school of astrologers who have been considerably influenced by Jung and his study of the unconscious. According to Mr. Dane Rudhyar in his very interesting treatise on *The Astrology of Personality* (Lucis Publishing Co., New York):

> Retrograde planets symbolize the turning back of the libido (psychic energy or life force) from the conscious into the unconscious. If a planet is retrograde, the function it represents is not activated for conscious co-operation. The psychic contents related to this function, instead of emerging directly in the conscious and thus influencing directly our behaviour, are thrown back temporarily into the unconscious. This does not mean necessarily that they are divested of their energy. They merge with other unconscious contents, then reappear later in the consciousness through the energy of the unconscious. The latter correspond to the planets Uranus, Neptune and Pluto (see pages 6 & 36).

If this suggestion of Mr. Rudhyar's is correct,[1] and it can only be proved so with the passing of time and numerous nativities collected to establish its veracity, the astrology of the future will have to develop along more intuitive lines than at present. For it is quite certain that the unconscious is far too vast and strange a territory to be subjected to the usual methods of astrological divination and calculations. Future American astrologers will probably evolve the new sixth sense of the Coming Race, whereby the super-

[1] I have tried this retrograde influence upon a nativity, which had puzzled me hitherto, and got astonishing results.

EXOTERIC ASTROLOGY

concious mind will apprehend truth through some new immediate insight of a subjective nature and apply this power to objective problems.

Mr. Rudhyar's ideas regarding the three outside planets, although considered from a different angle, tend to confirm my opinion regarding the influence of Uranus. Future students of astrology will doubtless realize that prophecies based *entirely* upon the planets influencing the conscious mind[1] may be considerably counteracted by the action of the three outside planets, which probably react mainly upon the conscious through upheavals in the unconscious, especially at this time of world unrest so evident everywhere.

[1] Mercury, Venus, Mars, Jupiter and Saturn.

BOOK II
ESOTERIC ASTROLOGY

Imagine the great heavenly bodies, stars and planets alike, ensouled by living Beings of inconceivable force and majesty and beauty.

Imagine, emanating from each of these living centres, vital currents which thrill through space.

Imagine these currents, which represent the life-essence of each of these mysterious stellar and planetary existences, radiating from them as mighty waves of colour, waves of sound, which although beyond the power of human sense to apprehend, nevertheless influence every particle and atom which they contact, every psychic and spiritual factor of Man's being.

The law of the Universe being absolute Unity, not one single emanation from the most far-off star-being but what must effect, to a greater or lesser degree, his brothers in space.

The Mystery of Life is indeed hidden in the stars, and it is for the true astrologer to decipher and interpret it to his fellows.—*Through the Eyes of the Masters.*

We whose work it is to gauge correctly and counteract, if necessary, the conflicting forces of Space, must know ahead which of the numerous astrological cycles and sub-cycles—all influencing and interpenetrating each other—is to predominate at a given time, and the approximate length of its duration. Just as a skilful mathematician makes his intricate calculations and retains them in his memory, so are we in our higher consciousness aware of the essentials of planetary problems covering vast periods of time, and concentrate upon those which are the most pressing at the moment.—*Ibid.*

Spiritual growth is only obtained through the transmutation of so-called malefic aspects.—*Adepts of the Five Elements.*

CHAPTER I

AN EASTERN SUBJECTIVE METHOD APPLIED TO AN ASTROLOGICAL PROBLEM

The sign Gemini rules the United States, the West of England, London, etc.—Zadkiel's *Ephemeris*, 1924.
The sign Leo rules France, Italy, etc.—*Ibid*.
The sign Virgo rules Paris, etc.—*Ibid*.

AFTER many years' practice and comparison Western astrologers have discovered that certain countries, counties and towns were affected adversely or otherwise by certain signs of the Zodiac according to varying conditions.

AN EASTERN ESOTERIC METHOD

Western astrology is based upon induction. Eastern astrology is derived from ancient traditions, either in book form or handed down from one astrologer to another from generation to generation. In India no one dreams of arguing over whether astrology is true or not, they accept it as a guide in their daily lives. Even the most illiterate family would not think of marrying a youth to a girl if their birth-charts proved inimical to each other.

ESOTERIC ASTROLOGY

Astrology in the East is thus above argument, and so the mind of the advanced astrologer is chiefly focused upon acquiring subjective intuition and applying it to daily life as a standardized accepted science.

In India the science of Yoga has been established and practised for centuries. It consists of the power to concentrate upon one thought or concept to the exclusion of every other. When this has been acquired with considerable effort after some years' practice, and the wandering mind brought back again and again to the fixed point or mental image, a new stage of mental control is encouraged. This is called Contemplation. Contemplation has three stages. Mr. Ernest Wood describes these in his remarkable book, *Concentration*, a practical course, which resembles Pelmanism, only it takes the mind further. These stages are as follows:

(1) The attention must be concentrated on the object.
(2) It must be stirred into activity with reference to that object alone.
(3) It must *remain actively centred* on the object while its own lower activities are successively suppressed.

Mr. Wood goes on to explain the process thus:

When the attention is no longer divided into parts by the activities of comparing, the mind will be moving as a whole, and will seem quite still, just as a spinning

AN EASTERN SUBJECTIVE METHOD

top may appear to stand still when it is in most rapid motion.

When the whole of your attention is occupied with the one thing, if you can raise your conception of the thing, without letting your attention stray to any other object, it is evident that you will be suppressing the lower types of vibration in your own mind and vivifying with your energy only the higher ; in short you will be raising the activity of your consciousness to a higher plane.

On this plane direct cognition is possible regarding any problem or point of interest, *provided* the lower mind or concrete brain approaches the problem without any personal or emotional bias.

Western psychology recognizes the possibility of obtaining illumination beyond the powers of the conscious mind through unconscious phenomena during sleep. Mr. Wood, in his pamphlet, *Personal Psychology and the Subconscious Mind*, gives an example of this procedure in the dream of Professor Agassiz related to Abercrombie's *Physiology*.

It happened that a portion of a fossil fish, protruding from a stone in one of the public gardens in Paris, was so unusual as to excite the Professor's special interest. He became anxious to classify the specimen, but could not do so because his utmost efforts of thought and imagination yielded him no picture of the full form of the fish, and the authorities would not permit him to break open the stone. At last he put the problem out of his mind as insoluble, until one night he suddenly awoke out of a dream in which he had clearly seen the missing portion of the fish. He jumped out of bed, got a pencil and paper, and sketched the form before it had time to fade, and afterwards satisfied himself

ESOTERIC ASTROLOGY

that his dream had given him what his *waking* logic and imagination failed to do.

Concentration and Contemplation, provided they are practised dispassionately, can provide the same illumination as the activities of the unconscious during sleep, only it is attained during the *waking* state.

When in India I practised this form of mental training, like many other people, and applied it to an astrological problem that happened to interest me. One day a remarkable astrologer, who had been working at the inner meanings of the twelve signs of the Zodiac, said he had arrived at a working hypothesis for all but the sign Aquarius. As the sign Aquarius is said to be the sign of the Coming Age, I decided, for that reason, to try and obtain inspiration with regard to it. I meditated for two years upon the inner meaning of that sign and arrived at some of the conclusions touched upon in my previous books.

All the following ideas written regarding the conscious, unconscious and superconscious minds in relation to the twelve signs of the Zodiac were arrived at through this Indian process of Contemplation during the last three years. These concepts are reinforced by various nativities as examples of my theory.

CHAPTER II

THE TWELVE SIGNS OF THE ZODIAC IN RELATION TO THE CONSCIOUS, UNCONSCIOUS AND SUPERCONSCIOUS MINDS

ACCORDING to a certain Rosicrucian initiate :
1. The first four signs (*Aries* the idealistic pioneer, *Taurus* the merchant, *Gemini* the journalist and *Cancer* the historian) are related to the conscious mind and so are chiefly extraverted.

2. The next four central signs are co-related to that centre called the " web of life " by Indian occultists and the " subconscious " or " unconscious " by Western psychologists. Thus *Leo*, patriotic display, *Virgo*, national commerce, *Libra*, balance of power, and *Scorpio*, race domination, alternatively prevail over the racial unconscious.

3. The last four signs, *Sagittarius* the fiery intuitive prophet, *Capricorn* the solitary Yogi or selfless server, *Aquarius* the Adept of the future, who leaves the circle of earthly desires for the upward spiral of mental abstract thought, and *Pisces*, he who has transmuted all personal

ESOTERIC ASTROLOGY

emotions into "universal compassion," in their *highest* sense, stand for the superconscious mind.

THE FOUR FIRST SIGNS AND THE CONSCIOUS MIND

Aries rules England and *Gemini* London, so the entry of *Neptune* into *Aries* and *Uranus* into *Gemini* preceding the occult thirty-five-year cycle that closed the nineteenth century was used to stimulate the advanced guard of the nation towards scientific research, social reforms and occult study.

A certain occultist, whose nativity combined the influence of both *Aries* and *Gemini*, inspired a group of men, who, in varying degrees, subordinated personal ambitions to national service.

North Devon, also under the sign *Gemini*, and partly selected for that reason, became an esoteric focus of mental fiery force. This Fire arose renewed—phoenix-like—from the ashes of earlier Elizabethan idealism and enterprise, activities that co-related this country with the United States, also ruled by *Gemini*.

An Englishman, also born under the influence of *Aries* and *Gemini*, living for a part of his life in Devon, helped to inspire these idealistic activities, both as a writer and a social worker.[1]

---

[1] Wherever a great initiate has endeavoured to realize for himself some of the fundamental truths of life, the ground about his dwelling-place and its environment takes on something of his magnetic and spiritual quality. It is not too

THE TWELVE SIGNS OF THE ZODIAC

The Socialist movement grew rapidly, reinforced as it was by a remarkable group of men, who had incarnated at the same period in order to attain inner unity and so work co-operatively.

As the esoteric activity of this group was both a subjective and ethical appeal, made through the elements fire and air, the occult power was polarized entirely in the higher centres. No one realized what the probable reactions would be in the race-unconscious, for very little was known about this centre at that time.

The Trade Unions, which had increased enormously during the twentieth century, became narrow and self-centred. Their pragmatical tendencies took on the particular characteristics of an afflicted *Virgo-Scorpio* combination. Hence their unity, instead of being used for the uplift of the entire working class, was ultimately employed merely to further their own ends.

The crest of this democratic wave became expressed through the nativity of J. Ramsay MacDonald, the first Labour prime minister, who had *Neptune* in *Aries,* ruler of the mid-heaven, in opposition to the *Sun* in its *fall* in *Libra*—dominating the end of the life—in square aspect to

much to say that the physical etheric conditions created by such an one may persist for several centuries after his death. Sometimes some of the most remarkable incidents of such a life can be seen by the clairvoyant, but only under favourable, i.e. impersonal, conditions."—From *Adepts of the Five Elements*.

the twelfth house of *self-undoing* containing Mars and Uranus influencing its cusp.[1]

At various times mankind has sought through societies and organizations great and small, to achieve some measure of unity. The Peace Pacts, the League of Nations and the various movements that aim at establishing peaceful relationships between various sections of the community, are examples of the struggling desire for co-operation. The apparent failure of all or any of those organizations merely indicates the inadequacy of the instrument or of those who wield it, not the inadequacy of the ensouling force, which would seem to grow through the failure of its forms.[2] For we must admit that the desire for peace and harmonious living between the nations is greater to-day than ever it was. But there is no need for dismay, even if John Brown's

---

[1] The twelfth house awakens the psychic mind and receptivity to the unseen worlds, therefore it is called the house of self-undoing. ♂ or ♅ placed here precipitates sudden and unexpected actions, the result of occult inspiration, and often causing obloquy if afflicted. This nativity, with its numerous afflictions involving cardinal signs, denotes internal strength expressed through external conflict. The late J. Ramsay MacDonald was an initiate, who obeyed an *inner order* when he sacrificed his party for the sake of the nation in the 1931 crisis. Nevertheless, the desire to remain too long in active work, the result of powerful planets in cardinal signs, frustrated the *occult* possibilities of the Sun in the fourth house, to be only attained through meditation upon fundamentals in complete seclusion.—*November*, 1937.

[2] The influence of ♅ and ♆ will bring other manifestations of this sort.

body is mouldering in the grave, his soul goes marching on.

THE FOUR CENTRAL SIGNS IN RELATION TO THE UNCONSCIOUS

National efforts at civic readjustment inevitably leading to a catastrophic upheaval in the unconscious were clearly evident in the French Revolution. As *Leo* rules France and *Virgo* Paris, these signs probably contained malefics at its inception. The entire nation oscillated between sublime ideals inspired by the new slogan, Liberty, Equality and Fraternity, and the perpetration of inhuman acts of cruelty. Idealism and ruthlessness were the outward and visible signs of an inner psychological upheaval and its inevitable reaction upon the racial unconscious.

This terrible development was anticipated by the mysterious individual the Comte de St. Germain.[1] Similarly his close follower, Cagliostro, foretold that a Corsican should temporarily " restore the power fallen from the hands of Louis XVI ".[2] This man of destiny was to act as both destroyer and regenerator in connexion with the aftermath of the *Leo-Virgo-Libra-Scorpio* upheaval.

[1] See *Souvenirs sur Marie Antoinette*, by the Comtesse d'Adhemar.
[2] See *The Story of Prophecy*, by Henry James Forman.

ESOTERIC ASTROLOGY

It is evident that Napoleon was aware of his destiny, for he constantly referred to ' his star " and was fully cognizant of astrological divination. During his most successful period he was advised by an able astrologer,[1] but lost touch with this man after the St. Helena incarceration.

His destiny carried him upon a wave of success at just the right psychological moment, without having to wait half a lifetime to achieve his ambitions. His horoscope, amazingly free from afflictions, has a well-aspected and powerful tenth house, reinforced by a magnetic subconscious *Virgo* combination in the eleventh, i.e. the *Sun* and *Mercury* in the tenth in *Leo*, supported by Mars conjunction *Neptune* in *Virgo* in the eleventh. The ascendant was *Libra* and contained *Jupiter* in *Scorpio*, but in opposition to *Uranus* in the seventh house, the last aspect causing his divorce, which directly effected the humiliating end indicated by the opposition of *Saturn* to the *Moon* from the tenth to the fourth houses respectively, from the signs of their detriment, *Cancer* and *Capricorn*.[2] Thus his *Leo-Virgo-Libra-Scorpio* sub-

[1] According to Cheiro, this astrologer was devoted to Napoleon, following him to Waterloo, with the intention of predicting disaster there. But officious military subordinates prevented the astrologer from seeing his patron. This man was killed on the field of battle—his destiny evidently fulfilled with Napoleon's defeat at Waterloo.

[2] Napoleon's nativity appears in Alan Leo's *1001 Notable Nativities*. Certain biographers have held the theory that

THE TWELVE SIGNS OF THE ZODIAC

conscious influence over others contained powerful planets in houses associated with public recognition and success at a time when the unconscious of the French race was open to the influence of ruthless men.

History repeats itself, as can be frequently seen by the astrologer. Both Hitler and Mussolini have powerful planets well aspected in the signs of the unconscious elevated. Mussolini has *Uranus* dominating the tenth house in *Virgo* in trine to *Neptune angular*, also swaying the unconscious and conscious minds of the Italians, through *Taurus* (speech). This combination is the most powerful in his nativity. His chief affliction is the *Moon* besieged by *Mars* (the ruler) and *Saturn* (destiny or fate) in the house of partners and open enemies. This aspect suggests that the former

Napoleon's parents added a year to his age by substituting their elder son's birthday for his, so that he might attend the military college in France. For even at an early age Napoleon revealed potential military genius. This would explain the fact that there are two birthdays ascribed to him—namely, 5th February, 1768, and 15th August, 1769. It is further suggested that Napoleon produced the earlier date at his marriage, for fear that army officials might discover the fraud practised upon the military college. Later on, his position as ruler of France being established, he reverted to his true birthday. If a horoscope can depict a type whose character and circumstances coincide with a particular Zodiacal sign, so conversely a powerful person should typify a *marked* example of certain Zodiacal characteristics. Napoleon both acted and looked like a Leo-Virgo-Scorpio type. The feeble introverted Aquarian nativity of 5th February, 1768, bore a far greater resemblance to his weak elder brother.

may not always remain subservient to his prevailing *Uranus*, whilst the latter may be found associated with the sign *Gemini* containing *Mars* in square to *Uranus* ruling the tenth house. Both

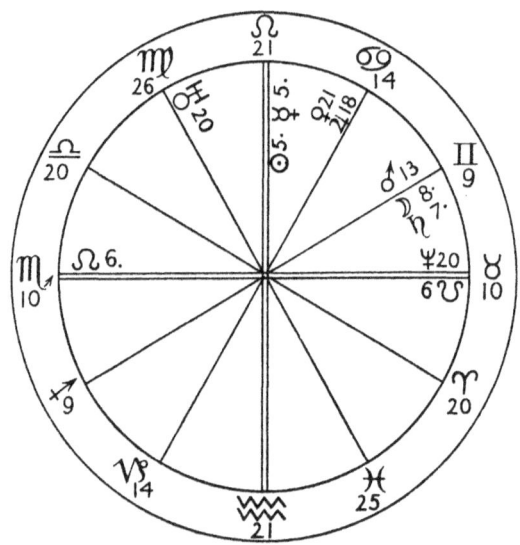

BENITO MUSSOLINI
Born at Doria, Italy, July 29th, 1883, 1.14 p.m.
(From Mr. Dane Rudhyar's *The Astrology of Personality*.)
The ascendant has been altered from 11 to 10 degrees rising because the Solar number is a more likely one to rule the ascendant.

his will and mind, the *Sun* and *Mercury* are in *Leo*, in the ninth house, free from affliction, and so able to dominate Italy ruled by *Leo*.

Hitler has *Uranus* rising in the twelfth house in sextile to *Saturn*, in *Leo* in the tenth house, accidentally dignified but in detriment, as in the

THE TWELVE SIGNS OF THE ZODIAC

case of Napoleon. *Saturn* afflicts both *Mars* and *Venus*.[1] It is interesting to note that the two signs of the unconscious, *Libra* and *Leo*, are angular and contain two planets, *Uranus* and *Saturn*, respectively associated with sudden upheavals and fatalistic enterprises of a dramatic nature.

With such a powerful combination of planets and signs that evidently have great power over the race-unconscious, these three men have been able to sway their various countrymen through an instinctive knowledge of mass psychology.

All three men suddenly appeared at times of national crisis, following a period of national humiliation or unrest. By reassuring crowds at frequent intervals, combined with gruelling hard work along executive lines, a temporary period of national self-assertion is inaugurated. That action and reaction are equal and opposite holds good with racial psychology as in everything else.[2]

---

[1] This aspect forms from the tenth to the seventh houses, indicating that whilst partners and co-workers placed Hitler in his present position, they can also become open enemies and pull him down again; a possibility if he lost the power of speech through the square aspect, as the sign Taurus contains Mars and Venus. This influence has already affected his voice and necessitated the skilful aid of a foreign throat specialist.

[2] The occult aftermath of a ruthless dictator often causes a serious vacuum of national etheric force. Both the first and last Napoleon had this effect upon the French. H. P. Blavatsky says somewhere that France never recovered from

ESOTERIC ASTROLOGY

Both Hitler and Mussolini demand an intense fiery *Leo* form of national expression, which may only be realized at the expense of international co-operation. A future development to be ultimately associated with the *opposite* sign *Aquarius*. As there is as yet no international moral sense nor an international police force to reinforce it, these two dictators are believed to be capable of precipitating a world crisis at any moment.

Like Napoleon, Mussolini has his own astrologer, whom he is *said* to consult with regard to every important decision. Hitler, too, was presaged by an astrologer in Germany, but that man was killed, under distinctly ruthless circumstances, after he had served his purpose by predicting Hitler's successful period (it is doubtful whether the French Revolution and its concomitant "the little corporal".

Put briefly, the occult failure of the French Revolution was caused by the Duke of Orleans becoming Grand Master of the most powerful French Masonic Lodge, and changing it from a non-political organization to a vast secret society owing *sworn* allegiance *only* to himself. Thus he completely destroyed the idealistic aims of French Freemasonry, inspired by the Comte de St. Germain and lesser initiates. Moreover, his badly conceived plan of ultimately ruling France, through discrediting his weak brother Louis XVI and Marie Antoinette, only caused their execution and his own combined with the entire political destruction of the French aristocracy ever since.

Further elucidation of this great occult experiment and of those that followed it, will only be made public when the present interest in mundane astrology leads on to a desire for something more recondite, associated with the influence of major and minor cycles.

THE TWELVE SIGNS OF THE ZODIAC

the afflicted *Saturn* in the mid-heaven was stressed).

The influence wielded by these two men carries

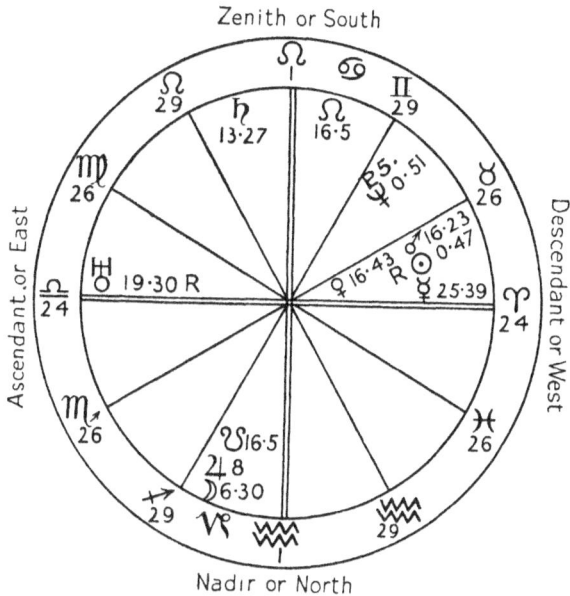

HITLER'S HOROSCOPE

6.17 p.m., April 20th, 1889, at Long. 13 E., Lat. 48 N.; from "Predication", June, 1936.

Mr. R. H. Naylor thinks the birthtime to be some "ten or fifteen minutes earlier". Probably the Solar number 19° was rising at birth, with Uranus upon the cusp of the ascendant. The other planets would remain in the same houses.

terrible responsibilities, for a powerful *Leo* can be disastrous to those lacking the *Virgo* discrimination or *Libra* balance required to counteract the fixed fiery force of the Solar sign.

The psychology of the future, based upon the

ESOTERIC ASTROLOGY

study of astrology, will stress the need of balancing the mind (*Virgo*) through (*Libra*) against the senses (*Scorpio*), thereby achieving poise and discrimination regarding public problems. History has revealed that those born with powerful planets elevated in the sign *Leo* rarely possess the power to laugh at themselves, although they have a strong sense of the dramatic and also of their own importance in the scheme of things.

THE FOUR FINAL SIGNS IN RELATION TO THE SUPERCONSCIOUS MIND

A new dispensation will be needed to follow the cycle of conflict between *Leonine* Fascism and *Aquarian* Communism, a conflict indicated by their mutual opposition aspect, stimulated by the turbulent sign *Scorpio* in adverse square to both. A sustained struggle considering the fixed signs involved. Both Fascism and Communism are different aspects of an arbitrary conception of national law imposed by the few upon the majority. For this reason they have often been compared with each other by the Press. Instinctively the serpent lurking in the symbolism of both *Leo* and *Aquarius* is feared and dreaded by many people who prefer a more equable realization of life. Unfortunately this more liberal conception lacks fire and co-operation, and so remains ineffective

THE TWELVE SIGNS OF THE ZODIAC

in a period of world chaos, invariably the concomitant of a changing age or dispensation.

As both Fascism and Communism are intensely of the present, they are likely to become exhausted in mutual conflict, seeing that both are endeavouring to become a dominating world force at the same time.[1] Even the most ardent adherents of either political organization would hardly go so far as to say either Fascism or Communism was the last word in race civilization or human endeavour.

It is therefore not difficult to predict that some master-mind will suddenly appear and create order out of chaos as others of a similar character have done before. But he will do so by being born under the sign *Sagittarius*, which is in benefic sextile and trine to *Aquarius* and *Leo* respectively. Thus will he harmonize the discordant elements produced by the clash between the two opposites. England under *Aries* and America under *Gemini*,

---

[1] The above prognostication, written last summer, is reinforced this month by that intuitive astrologer Mr. Edward Lyndoe, who writes for "The People" every week. On being asked to give his views on the possibilities of a world conflict based on Fascism v. Communism, he replies:—"I answer with a positive no, within the next 6 years both Fascism and Communism, as we know them, will have been radically modified and materially weakened. There will never be a Fascist Empire on any scale, nor will Communism succeed in any large conquests."—Edward Lyndoe in "The People", November 21st, 1937.

both in benefic aspect to *Aquarius* and *Leo*, may do much as nations to arbitrate at this period.

Alan Leo, the intuitive astrologer, says somewhere that whereas *Aries* resembles the private soldier and *Leo* the captain, *Sagittarius* can become the general who foresees victory arising out of what threatens to become inevitable defeat, through some swift decision made at a critical moment in the battle. There is a legend regarding Wellington that illustrates this point. Whilst gazing at Napoleon across the field of Waterloo, he saw the French general give an order to his A.D.C. In some intuitive way Wellington divined what it was and instantly conceived another strategy of his own to counteract it. Be that as it may, minds of the same type, both intuitive and daring, will be needed in the near future if civilization is not to perish entirely.

Being both fiery and mutable, evolved *Sagittarians* possess the power of swift transference of consciousness, from the intuitive subjective state direct to the physical brain. Hence *Sagittarius* is the sign of the prophet. Like all the mutable signs, its dual nature can harmonize the objective and subjective qualities of the mind through one vivid flash of inspired intuition.

Many minds of this type will be needed in the near future as well as *Aquarian* psychological pioneers, *Pisces* welfare workers and *Capricornian*

THE TWELVE SIGNS OF THE ZODIAC

exponents of Yoga, suited to *modern* conditions. These must work side by side as specialists in the Coming Age.

The conflict arising from emotional and mental racial conceptions of such arbitrary types as Fascism and Communism (*as at present conceived*) [1] will create a world-condition of emotional and mental suspense. An inevitable reaction must follow. The younger generation of that period will be in resistance to existing conditions and demand something different from either conception. Just as the Edwardians ridiculed the Victorians and the Georgians satirized the Edwardians, so will the future *Sagittarians* become devastating critics of any and every attempt to dominate or exploit the masses by arbitrary conceptions of rulership. Intensely individual in mind, they will overthrow all efforts to mould their minds, and will seek an inner inspiration for their actions, no matter what the cost.

Those born under this sign resent intensely having either their mental or physical liberty curtailed within arbitrary or outworn rules or conventions. Thus this period of the future will need inspired *Aquarians* to propound new *Uranian* methods of inner development, which can be fully

---

[1] ♅ △ ♆ may inspire leading minds, responsive to their influence, to anticipate this deadlock by an unexpected Uranian gesture of a constructive and international nature.

realized through individual effort and *self-discipline*. Later on these *Uranian* forms of Yoga, applied to the physical consciousness, will become universally recognized during the next two centuries. Similarly the more political *Uranian* mind of the future will be applied to the problem of pooling the world's resources and achieving international co-operation. Thus the *Aquarian* Age will come to fruition.

Before this desirable development can be achieved, the educational system of every country will have to be altered and an international point of view fostered rather than a purely national one. Without a broader and more impersonal conception of education, national egoism, masquerading as patriotism, will continue to arise volcanically from the race-unconscious, thereby plunging the world into war with all its attendant misery and chaos.

The main objective of reviving the study of astrology in the West, is to teach man to know himself. This can only be achieved along *impersonal* lines, with the mind standing clear of the emotions and ambitions. As we gaze with awe upon our horoscopes, which indicate the sum-total of numerous past undisciplined lives, we realize the basic truth that as we sow in one life, so do we reap in a later one. Our limitations are the result of some moral deficiency or our own reckless actions, our abilities are the fruit of earlier efforts. This is the old law of Saturn, ruler of Aquarius, which will be associated with the Coming Age.

Later on the advanced guard of humanity will be learning to respond to the highest influence of the far-off worlds, Uranus and Neptune. Having learnt that abuse of physical power is not worth while, a desire for selfless service will arise and slowly become a spiritual directing force in the world. This form of spiritual development has been ably expressed in that inspired work, *Agni Yoga* :

> The spheres of psychic energy penetrate all obstacles. All physical and mechanical manifestations have no value in comparison with the finest energy, the whole future is founded upon the highest energies, upon the return of coarse matter into the domain of light. . . .
> Few are the trusted builders who with self-denial accept the thought of space into the chalice of the heart. They are not frightened at being scorched by the fires of the *far-off worlds*.

Thus the higher side of Sagittarius will be brought into focus upon this plane. Gradually those who have been daring pioneers of speed in this world, will, in future lives, become equally daring in the non-physical realms. In spirit and in thought they will swiftly co-relate the higher consciousness with the life of the physical plane. Their freedom from inhibitions, conventions and outworn traditions will give them affinity with the forces of the New Era, the Aquarian powers of the Air. Thus will the ancient prophecy regarding the new earth Age be fulfilled : " Behold, I make all things New ! "[1]

[1] This ancient prophecy is associated with another which refers to that time, which " shall test the Very Elect ". Surely this cryptic combination implies a repolarization on all planes ? Which can only be fully experienced in bodies open solely to the forces of the future ?

Mrs. Alice Bailey says somewhere that some time during this century certain Adepts will emerge from Their obscurity. But obviously bodies maintained through *Venusian* currents of force at great altitudes, are quite unsuited to a world responding chiefly to the affects of *Uranus* and *Neptune*. Through psychological identification with a few of the more advanced of the younger generation, They will experience their problems and divine how to overcome them. For These trusted builders are not frightened of being scorched by the fires of the *far-off worlds*.

APPENDIX

AN AMERICAN NATIVITY

THE chart taken is that of the Duchess of Windsor. The birth took place at 5.30 a.m. Eastern Standard Time, on June 19th, 1896, at Baltimore, Lat. 39° 16' N., Long.

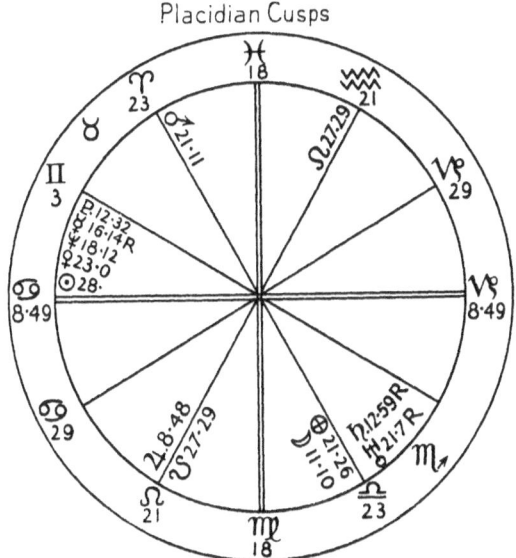

THE DUCHESS OF WINDSOR'S NATIVITY
About 5.30 a.m., June 19th, 1896, Baltimore.

76° 41' W. The Sidereal Time on that day was 5·49, and on the day previous 5·45.
Greenwich Time. Eastern Standard Time is five hours later

APPENDIX

than Greenwich. The equivalent Greenwich Time was thus 1.30 a.m.

Local Time. The Longitude is 76° 41'. At the rate of four minutes a degree this is equivalent to 5 hr. 6 min. 40 sec. The Standard Time being only five hours different from Greenwich, the true *Local* Time was 6 min. 40 sec. earlier than the time given, or 5.23.20 a.m. The time elapsing to noon was thus 6 hr. 36 min. 40 sec.

The calculation proceeds:

Sidereal Time .	5	49	
Add . . .	24		
	29	49	
Deduct time elapsing	6	36	40
	23	12	20
Deduct correction at 10 sec. per hour elapsing		1	6
	23	11	14

An alternative calculation would be:

Sidereal Time .	5	45	on previous day.
Add time elapsed	17	23	20 from previous noon.
Add correction at 10 sec. per hour elapsed		2	54
	23	11	14

The Table of Houses for Lat. 39 N. gives an Ascendant of eight degrees of Cancer for this time, and the signs on the other cusps are similarly read off.

The Planetary positions for a Greenwich Time of 10.30 a.m. are next obtained from the ephemeris for the year, and the " map " is then complete apart from the calculation of aspects.

(It will be noted that although the calculations have included minutes and seconds, they are really based entirely on the birth time, which was only given in round minutes, a fact which always suggests an *approximate* time rather than an *exact* time. On general considerations it is extremely im-

AN AMERICAN NATIVITY

probable that the *exact* time of birth is ever, or can ever be, recorded.)

THE NATIVITY OF THE DUCHESS OF WINDSOR

According to *Astrology* (March, April, May) the editor has " received unimpeachable information " that the birth time of the Duchess of Windsor's nativity " was at 5.30 a.m., E.S.T., at Baltimore, U.S.A., which yields an ascendant of 9½ Cancer ". The June number of that magazine contained a nativity of the duchess cast for 5.23.19 a.m., L.M.T., which gives 8.49 Cancer rising. Mr. Bray's article upon this remarkable nativity further states " that the hour of birth was between 5.30 and 6 a.m." This chart is cast for 5.30 a.m., although the duchess resembles the Scorpio decanate type rather than the Cancerian or first decanate. Probably she had 9½ Cancer rising, thereby expressing a combination of Mars and the Sun in terms of numerology. In any case the planets are in the same house position. Students of astrology might do well to compare the first with the second decanate influences as described in *How to Judge a Nativity*, p. 92. According to Alan Leo, the first decanate brings out the Moon's influence and the second that of Mars, whose position should be noted. In this case Mars has probably had more influence up to the age of forty, whilst the Moon will have greater effect towards the end of life, owing to its position in the fourth house.

Mars is elevated by house and strong by sign, being in Aries. It gives fluent speech and an alert, independent spirit. Of this position Sepharial writes :

> In military life, success ; in other fields of work, danger of discredit. The native suffers from slander and his life is filled with turmoil and strife. Desire for conquest and a spirit of freedom spur the native to outstrip his powers and exhaust his energies. The native is often quarrelsome, but quite as often the subject of constant fault-finding and criticism.—*A Manual of Astrology*, p. 44.

This powerful position of Mars is reinforced by Saturn and Uranus in the Martian sign Scorpio and in the fifth house, which is a spectacular one frequently bringing fame or notoriety.

The planet Uranus placed here denotes remarkable love affairs and is not fortunate as regards children, whilst Saturn

APPENDIX

denotes hindrances, delay or disappointment in love affairs and is not good for speculation, favouring only safe investments connected with land, mines or buildings. In this case Saturn square Jupiter from the house of speculation to the house of finance according to Alan Leo "threatens loss of money, credit and the life may be subject to periods of great opposition, reversals and very heavy losses". Fortunately this is the only serious affliction in the nativity.

The most remarkable feature of the chart is the concentration of no less than five influences in the twelfth house, indicating physical restrictions imposing periods of retirement and introspection. As these influences are free from affliction, the duchess probably does not seek to escape the limitations of the twelfth house and may receive considerable benefit later on in life along twelfth-house lines through the benefic trine the Moon receives from Pluto, Mercury and Neptune. So potent, indeed, is her twelfth-house influence, that the powerful conjunctions therein have changed the whole trend of her husband's career, altering it from one of intense activity to an immediate retirement from all public life. This has been achieved through the conjunction his Neptune and Jupiter (ruling the end of his life) makes to her twelfth-house Neptune and Mercury. In this way each nativity reinforces the other through airy trines formed from introspective subjective houses. According to Alan Leo, the conjunction between Jupiter and Neptune sometimes signifies "precocious occult genius, recovered lore from higher planes, remembrance of past lives". As this aspect rules the *end* of life for the Duke of Windsor, his future contains strange possibilities for subjective or mystic realizations.

SOME FURTHER NOTES ON SETTING UP A CHART

VARIOUS " Times " have to be dealt with and understood. They are as follows :

SIDEREAL TIME is star time, and the sidereal day represents one complete rotation of the earth in relation to any fixed star. Between year and year, there is a maximum difference of only six minutes for the same date in different years.

SOLAR TIME is Sun time, and the Solar day represents one complete rotation of the earth in relation to the Sun : the earth's orbital movement is slightly irregular, and the consequent irregularity in Solar time is corrected in—

GREENWICH TIME, which is almost universally adopted as the standard by which time in all parts of the world is set.

LOCAL TIME is Greenwich time, adjusted to Longitude East or West by addition or subtraction at the rate of four minutes to every degree, or fifteen degrees to one hour.

STANDARD TIME or ZONE TIME is Greenwich time, adjusted by a round number of hours, and applied to a whole country, or a considerable zone of a large country, irrespective of exact longitude. The United States of America has three *Zone* times, Eastern Zone time being five hours later than Greenwich : noon in this Zone is thus 5 p.m. at Greenwich. The whole of India has one *Standard* time which is five-and-a-half hours earlier than Greenwich : noon in India is thus 7 a.m. at Greenwich. *This Standard or Zone time is the* CLOCK TIME *which is usually given to the Astrologer as the birth time.*

SUMMER TIME needs no definition : but it should be remembered that it was introduced in different years in different countries, and is in operation between different dates. Raphael's *Ephemeris* gives details for the United Kingdom. For other countries special tables must be consulted.

The Golden Rule in casting a horoscope is as follows :

LOCAL time is used to calculate CUSPS of Houses.

GREENWICH time is used to calculate positions of PLANETS.

APPENDIX

In the case of births where Greenwich time is in force, only two steps are necessary : the adjustment for longitude at the rate of four minutes for each degree and a small addition (which has not previously been mentioned) of ten seconds for each hour elapsed between previous noon and time of birth in Local time.

In other cases, a further step is necessary in the correction of the difference between Standard time and Greenwich time. The method of effecting this is shown in detail in the example given later.

TABLES OF HOUSES

A table of houses is only correct for the particular degree of Latitude for which it is drawn up. Raphael's *Ephemeris* gives tables for London, Liverpool and New York. The London table is applicable to such places as Brighton, Brussels, Cologne, Leipzig, and Solingen, whilst the Liverpool table covers Berlin, Dublin, Stettin and Konigsberg. If extreme accuracy is required, a table of houses for the actual degree of latitude should be used, but for practical purposes the London table can be used for the South and Midlands, and the Liverpool table for the North. Whatever table is used, for a given Sidereal time the cusp of the tenth house will be the same.

The Table of Houses for North Latitudes can be used for South Latitudes by adding twelve hours to the Sidereal time for birth : and by using the table for the same Latitude North as the birth is South, but *reversing* the sign shown.

LATITUDE, LONGITUDE, AND DECLINATION

The Latitude of a Planet is its distance above or below the line of the Ecliptic. This is not often used in Astrology.

The Longitude of a Planet is its position measured in degrees along the Ecliptic, from its first point at Aries 0, and then on throughout the twelve signs.

The Declination of a Planet is its distance above or below the Equator. It is said to be North in the former case and South in the latter. The Parallel of Declination (symbol P) occurs when two planets are equal in declination, irrespective of whether they are North or South or both, and is regarded as an aspect similar to the conjunction.

SOME FURTHER NOTES

CALCULATING THE PLANETS' POSITIONS

Where extreme accuracy is desired, the movement of the planets between the Greenwich noon position shown in the *Ephemeris* and the Greenwich time of birth must be allowed for.

In later *Ephemerides*, a separate table is provided showing the daily motion of the Sun, Moon, Mars, Venus and Mercury. Where the table is not available, the daily movement is the difference between the noon position on the day of birth and the noon position for the day preceding or subsequent to the day of birth according as the birth time was before or after noon ; this is obtained by subtraction, and then apportioned according to the time elapsed and added to or subtracted from the noon position. If the time elapsed is a simple fraction of twenty-four hours, the calculation can be done mentally. In other cases the table of proportionate logarithms incorporated in the *Ephemeris* can be used. It is unnecessary to detail the method which is given at the foot of the table.

If the planet is *retrograde*, differences must be added instead of subtracted, and vice versa.

EPHEMERIDES AND TABLES

Reference has already been made to the *Ephemerides* issued by Raphael. Attention might also be drawn to a small volume entitled *Planetosophy*, Vol. 1, which can be obtained, like all other astrological books and requirements, from Mr. J. S. Watkins, 23, Cecil Court, Charing Cross Road, London, W.C.2. This contains full details of Local and Standard Times, Tables of Houses for all Latitudes, and a condensed ephemeris for the years 1886 to 1935 inclusive, together with logarithmic tables and other data.

INDEX

Italics indicate nativities mentioned in the text.
A small " n " indicates a footnote.

ADEPT, 31, 35, 198 n.
Agni Yoga, 197
Air, Element of, 11
Airy Signs, 55
Alfonso, King, 82
Angles, 7
Angular Houses, 7
Animal Signs, 12
Applying Aspects, 26
Aquarian Age, 31, 104, 110, 112, 113, 139, 196-8
Aquarius, 11, 32 n., 55, 140, 181, 192, 193, 194, 195, 197
  decanates of, 100
Aries, 9, 54, 181, 182, 183, 193, 194
  decanates of, 65
Ascendant, 7
  how to find, 18-20
  progressed, 146
Aspects, applying, 26
  calculation of, 24
  conjunction, 38
  definition of, 24
  meaning of, 27
  separating, 26

BAILEY, Alice, 198
Barrie, Sir J. M., 76
Besant, Annie, 32 n., 156, 157 n., 160 n.
Blavatsky, H. P., 32 n., 78, 112 n., 189 n.
Body, in relation to Zodiac, 12
Boulanger, Gen., 37 n.

CADENT Houses, 9
Cagliostro, 185
Cancer, 10, 56, 112 n., 181
  decanates of, 74
  (disease), 141
Capricorn, 10, 57, 181, 192, 194
  decanates of, 96
Cardinal Signs, 11
Charles I, 80
Charles II, 82
Chopin, 82
Communism, 192, 193, 195
Conscious mind, xiv, 112, 139, 174, 181, 182
Constellations, 4
Constitutions, 11
Contemplation, 178

207

INDEX

Cosmic Rays, 35
Crawford, Joan, 89
Cusps, 7
Cycles, 110 n.

DECANATES, 62
Declination, 204
Descendant, 8
Detriment, 15
Diet, 140
Directional Astrology, 149 n.
Diseases of Signs, 58
Disraeli, 96
Dragon's Head, Tail, 29
Dreams, 127
Dunne, J., 110

EARTH, Element of, 11
Earthy Signs, 57
Eclipses, 29, 150
Education, future Aquarian, 196
Elements, 11, 53
Elizabeth Tudor, 96
Emotions and Mind, 161
Ephemeris, 18, 203–5
Equinoxes, Precession of, 104
Eugenie, Empress, 94
Exaltation, 15

FALL, 15
Fascism, 192, 193, 195
Feminine Signs, 12
Fiery Signs, 54
Fire, Element of, 11
Fixed Signs, 11
French Revolution, 185, 190
Fruitful Signs, 12

GEMINI, 9, 55, 177, 181, 182, 188, 193
  decanates of, 72
  universal diffused interest of, 101, 113
Gladstone, 97

HAPSBURG, facial formation, 83
Healing, 139
Health and Planets, 59
  and Hyleg, 137
Hitler, 86, 131 n., 160 n., 187, 188, 190, 191
Houses, angular, 7
  cadent, 9
  characteristics of, 9
  opposing, 155, 156, 159
  Planets in, 114
  Tables of, 19, 200, 204
Human Signs, 12
Hyleg, 137

INTERCEPTED Signs, 20, 25
Internationalism, necessity for, 190, 196

JUNG, 108, 173
Jupiter, aspects of, 40, 44, 49
  influence of, 33
  in Houses, 114, 116, 117, 119, 123, 124, 126, 129, 131, 133, 135
  in relation to Body, 15
  in transit, 144
  rising, 60

KRISHNAMURTI, 156, 157 n., 158

208

INDEX

LATITUDE, 204
League of Nations, 184
Leo, 10, 54, 185, 186, 187 n.,
    189, 191, 192, 193, 194
  decanates of, 78
Leo, Alan, 52, 194, 201, 202
Libra, 10, 55, 185, 186, 189, 191
  decanates of, 84
Longitude, 204
Luminaries and Signs, 52

MACDONALD, J. Ramsay, 183
  184 n.
McCrea, Joel, 92
Mars, aspects of, 41, 45, 50
  influence of, 32
  in Houses, 115, 116, 118,
    119, 121, 123, 125, 129,
    132, 134, 135
  in relation to Body, 14
  rising, 61
Masculine Signs, 12
Mercury, aspects of, 46, 51
  influence of, 30
  in Houses, 115, 116, 118,
    120, 121, 123, 125, 127,
    129, 132, 134, 136
  in relation to Body, 14
  rising, 61–2
Meridian, 7
Mid-heaven, 7
Mind and emotions, 161, 162
  conscious, unconscious,
    superconscious, 181
Moon, aspects of, 39
  influence of, 29, 52, 53 n.
  in Houses, 115, 117, 118,
    120, 122, 123, 124, 126,
    129, 131, 133, 135

Moon, in relation to Body,
  15
  rising, 62
Mozart, 82
Mussolini, 89, 131 n., 160 n.,
  187, 188, 190
Mutable Signs, 11
Mutual Reception, 26

NADIR, 8
Napoleon I, 86, 131 n., 169,
  186, 187, 189, 190
Napoleon III, 94, 189 n.
Neptune, aspects of, 38, 42, 46
  influence of, 6, 32 n., 36,
    53 n., 112, 164, 197
  in Houses, 114, 115, 117,
    119, 120, 122, 124, 126,
    128, 130, 133, 135
  in relation to Body, 14
  in transit, 144
  rising, 59
Nodes, 29

OPPOSING Houses, 155, 156,
  159, 160
Opposition, 25

PERIODS, Planetary, 145
Personality and Moon, 29
Pisces, 11, 56, 110, 113, 140,
  181, 194
  decanates of, 105
  past method of healing, 139
Planets, affinities, 15
  and Health, 59
  detriment of, 15
  exaltation of, 15
  fall of, 15

INDEX

Planets, House rulership of, 9
  mutual reception, 26
  periods of, 145
  retrograde, 172
  rising, 59
  symbols, 6
  void of Course, 26
Pluto, influence of, 5
Precession of Equinoxes, 104 n.
Progressed Horoscope, 141
Psycho-analysis, 112, 113, 140
Psychology, crowd, 189
  of Future, 191, 192

QUADRUPLICITIES, 24
Quincunx, 24

RAPHAEL, 5, 6 n., 149, 150
Retrograde Planets, 172, 173
" Ring-pass-not ", 34
Rosebery, Lord, 105
Rudhyar, Dane, 6 n., 173, 174

SAGITTARIUS, 10, 54, 181, 193, 194, 195, 197
  decanates of, 92
St. Germain, Comte de, 185, 190 n.
Saturn, aspects of, 40, 44, 48
  influence of, 34, 140, 141, 197
  in Houses, 114, 116, 117, 119, 121, 123, 124, 126, 129, 131, 133, 135
  in relation to Body, 14
  in transit, 144
  rising, 60

Scorpio, 10, 56, 102, 103 n., 107, 110, 185, 186, 187 n., 192
  decanates of, 89
Secondary Progressions, 145
Semi-sextile, 24
Semi-square, 24
Separating Aspects, 26
Sepharial, 53, 210
Serpent symbolism, 102 n., 192
Sesqui-quadrate, 24
Sextile, 24
Signs, affinities with Planets, 15
  characteristics of, 54
  diseases of, 58
  division into elements, 11, 53–7
  in relation to psychology, 181–97
  ruling countries, 177
  symbols of, 4
Solar system, 4
Square, 24
Succedent Houses, 7
Sun, aspects of, 41, 46, 50
  influence of, 28, 52, 53 n.
  in Houses, 115, 116, 118, 120, 122, 123, 125, 127, 130, 132, 134, 136
  rising, 61
Superconscious mind, xiv, 112, 113, 182, 192
Symbols, aspectual, 24
  Planetary, 6
  Zodiacal, 4
Synthesis, the art of, 152–64

INDEX

TAURUS, 9, 57, 181
  decanates of, 69
Time, Greenwich, Sidereal, Summer, 19, 203
Transits, 143-4
Trine, 24
Triplicities, 24
Twelve Rising Signs and decanate influences, 64-113

UNCONSCIOUS mind, xiv n., 36 n., 112 n., 113, 139, 140, 174, 179, 181, 183, 185, 186, 187, 189
Uranus, aspects of, 39, 43, 47
  influence of, 6 n., 32 n., 34, 35, 53 n., 112, 164, 197
  in Houses, 114, 116, 117, 119, 121, 122, 124, 126, 128, 131, 133, 135
  in relation to Body, 14
  in transit, 144
  rising, 60

VEGETARIANISM, 141
Venus, aspects of, 46
  influence of, 31, 157
Venus, in Houses, 115, 116, 118, 120, 121, 123, 125, 127, 129, 132, 134, 136
  in relation to Body, 14
  rising, 61
Virgo, 10, 57, 141, 181, 185, 186, 187, 191
  decanates of, 80

WAGNER, 165, 167, 168, 170, 171
Water, Element of, 11
Watery Signs, 56
"Web of Life", 112, 181
Wellington, 194
Wells, H. G., 88, 108
Wilde, Oscar, 37 n., 131 n.
Windsor, Duchess of, 199, 200, 201
  Duke of, 155, 202
Wood, Ernest, 178, 179

YOGA, 178, 195, 196

ZENITH, 8
Zodiac, definition of, 4
  in relation to Body, 12
  symbols of, 4

ARIES   TAURUS   GEMINI   CANCER

SCORPIO SAGITTARIUS

Better books make better astrologers.
Here are some of our other titles:

AstroAmerica's Daily Ephemeris, 2010-2020
AstroAmerica's Daily Ephemeris, 2000-2020
   - both for Midnight. *Compiled & formatted by David R. Roell*

Al Biruni
The Book of Instructions in the Elements of the Art of Astrology, *1029 AD, translated by R. Ramsay Wright*

Derek Appleby
Horary Astrology: The Art of Astrological Divination

E.H. Bailey
The Prenatal Epoch

Joseph Blagrave
Astrological Practice of Physick

C.E.O. Carter
The Astrology of Accidents
An Encyclopaedia of Psychological Astrology
Essays on the Foundations of Astrology
The Principles of Astrology, *Intermediate no. 1*
Some Principles of Horoscopic Delineation, *Intermediate no. 2*
Symbolic Directions in Modern Astrology
The Zodiac and the Soul

Charubel & Sepharial
Degrees of the Zodiac Symbolized, *1898*

H.L. Cornell
Encyclopaedia of Medical Astrology

Nicholas Culpeper
Astrological Judgement of Diseases from the Decumbiture of the Sick, *1655, and,* **Urinalia**, *1658*

Dorotheus of Sidon
Carmen Astrologicum, *c. 50 AD, translated by David Pingree*

Nicholas deVore
Encyclopedia of Astrology

Firmicus Maternus
Ancient Astrology Theory & Practice: Matheseos Libri VIII, *c. 350 AD, translated by Jean Rhys Bram*

Margaret Hone
The Modern Text-Book of Astrology

William Lilly
Christian Astrology, books 1 & 2, *1647*
  The Introduction to Astrology, Resolution of all manner of questions.
Christian Astrology, book 3, *1647*
  Easie and plaine method teaching how to judge upon nativities.

Alan Leo
The Progressed Horoscope, *1905*

Jean-Baptiste Morin
The Cabal of the Twelve Houses Astrological
  translated by George Wharton, edited by D.R. Roell

Claudius Ptolemy
Tetrabiblos, *c. 140 AD, translated by J.M. Ashmand*

Vivian Robson
Astrology and Sex
Electional Astrology
Fixed Stars & Constellations in Astrology
A Beginner's Guide to Practical Astrology
A Student's Text-Book of Astrology, Vivian Robson Memorial Edition

Diana Roche
The Sabian Symbols, A Screen of Prophecy

Richard Saunders
The Astrological Judgement and Practice of Physick, *1677*

Sepharial
The Manual of Astrology, the Standard Work
Primary Directions, a definitive study
Sepharial On Money. *For the first time in one volume, complete texts:*
  • **Law of Values**
  • **Silver Key**
  • **Arcana, or Stock and Share Key** — *first time in print!*

James Wilson, Esq.
Dictionary of Astrology

H.S. Green, Raphael & C.E.O. Carter
Mundane Astrology: *3 Books, complete in one volume.*

If not available from your local bookseller, order directly from:
The Astrology Center of America
207 Victory Lane
Bel Air, MD 21014

on the web at:
http://www.astroamerica.com

www.ingramcontent.com/pod-product-compliance
Lightning Source LLC
Chambersburg PA
CBHW020354170426
43200CB00005B/166